Riverside Junior High School
10910 Eller Road
Fishers, Indiana 46038

Women of Achievement

Tyra Banks

Women of Achievement

Abigail Adams

Susan B. Anthony

Tyra Banks

Clara Barton

Hillary Rodham Clinton

Marie Curie

Ellen DeGeneres

Diana, Princess of Wales

Helen Keller

Sandra Day O'Connor

Georgia O'Keeffe

Nancy Pelosi

Rachael Ray

Eleanor Roosevelt

Martha Stewart

Venus and Serena Williams

Women of Achievement

Tyra Banks

MODEL AND TALK SHOW HOST

Anne M. Todd

CHELSEA HOUSE
PUBLISHERS

An imprint of Infobase Publishing

TYRA BANKS

Chelsea House
An imprint of Infobase Publishing
132 West 31st Street
New York, NY 10001

Library of Congress Cataloging-in-Publication Data
Todd, Anne M.
 Tyra Banks: Model and Talk Show Host / by Anne M. Todd.
 p. cm. — (Women of achievement)
 Includes bibliographical references and index.
 ISBN 978-1-60413-462-9 (hardcover)
 1. Banks, Tyra—Juvenile literature. 2. Models (Persons)—United States—Biography—Juvenile literature. 3. African American television personalities—United States—Biography—Juvenile literature. 4. Television personalities—United States—Biography—Juvenile literature. I. Title. II. Series.

 HD6073.M77B3663 2009
 746.9'2092—dc22
 [B]
                                2009009915

Series design by Erik Lindstrom
Cover design by Ben Peterson and Alicia Post

Printed in the United States of America

Bang EJB 10 9 8 7 6 5 4 3 2 1

This book is printed on acid-free paper.

CONTENTS

Goodbye to Runway

Nearly 7 million viewers watched the holiday-inspired Tenth Annual Victoria's Secret Fashion Show on television in 2005. All eyes watched as a curvy, well-proportioned model strutted the runway, dressed in a black satin corset and 5-inch (12.7 centimeters, or cm) heels. The woman modeling was Tyra Banks—and she looked poised and self-assured. A shimmering diamond necklace hung around her neck. She wore an elaborate, feathery, costume-like set of black wings attached to her back. The enormous wings trailed behind her down the runway. Angel wings—whether they are giant or tiny; black, white, or purple—are a trademark of Victoria's Secret. They were part of the look that distinguished the Victoria's Secret "Angels," or most elite models.

Banks's 5-foot, 10-inch (178 cm) frame and her striking gait exuded complete confidence and demanded attention as she made her way down the length of the catwalk. Her caramel-colored skin glowed; her silky-straight, waist-length brown hair tumbled around her; and her intense emerald eyes looked straight ahead with a focused purpose and determination. When Banks reached the end of the runway, her eyes softened and she flashed one of her famous smiles, shifted her weight from one hip to the other, and briefly held the pose. Then Tyra Banks turned and walked away—but tonight's walks were different from her previous walks. This time, Banks was taking her final jaunts up and down the runway. Tyra Banks was walking away from runway modeling altogether.

When supermodel Tyra Banks announced she was retiring from modeling, she declared the end-of-the-year Victoria's Secret Fashion Show to be her last walk on the runway. Victoria's Secret had helped shape Banks's career.

The company had come a long way from its modest beginnings. Roy Raymond had founded Victoria's Secret in San Francisco, California, back in 1977. He had wanted to create a store where men would not feel embarrassed to purchase lingerie, as he had when he tried to buy lingerie for his wife. Five years later, he sold his company, which then consisted of four stores and a mail-order catalog, to The Limited. Keeping the name Victoria's Secret, in the 1990s, the company began hiring some of the most popular models to pose for their catalogs and ad campaigns. The Victoria's Secret Angels modeled only the newest collections of lingerie. One of those original Angels was Tyra Banks. Lingerie sales soared.

Banks had been modeling Victoria's Secret lingerie for about 10 years. Her work with the company had helped earn Banks supermodel status. Through Victoria's Secret, Tyra Banks had made a name for herself in the commercial modeling industry. Now, joining Banks at this 2005 fashion show at the New York State Armory in Manhattan, were the other original Victoria's Secret Angels: Gisele Bundchen, Laetitia Casta, Helena Christensen, Yasmeen Ghauri, Izabel Goulart, Heidi Klum, Karen Moulder, Daniela Pestova, Maria Ines Rivero, Rebecca Romijn, and Stephanie Seymour.

The original Angels worked the runway. Between sets, they would jockey for space backstage to change quickly into their next costume. Stylists were on hand to help the models with their changes. Stylists also pinned, tucked, adjusted, and altered lingerie as needed. For one of Banks's catwalks, she wore a blue and purple paisley bra with a purple string bikini bottom. She wore a sheer, sparkly purple cape edged with dark purple boa trim, which flowed behind her as she walked. In a third trip down the runway, Banks modeled red lingerie. Multicolored ribbons hung in front of a red cape draped over her left arm. The ribbons and cape reached to the ground. Similar, shorter ribbons tipped with gold bells and baubles wrapped around Banks's waist. In her right hand, Banks carried a long silver staff with a glittering "V" (for Victoria) at the top. Banks, carrying the staff like a ringleader, led the other Angels down the runway.

At this show, a new generation of Victoria's Secret Angels were introduced: Alessandra Ambrosio, Selita

DID YOU KNOW?

Tyra Banks earned $4 million each year modeling lingerie for Victoria's Secret. When walking runways in New York or Paris, Banks could earn $50,000 a day.

Tyra Banks walks the runway for the last time at the Victoria's Secret Fashion Show in New York City in 2005.

Ebanks, Miranda Kerr, Doutzen Kroes, Karolina Kurkova, Adriana Lima, and Marisa Miller. Each model, past and present, took turns walking the runway, modeling the new collections of lingerie. From the sidelines, big names in both the fashion and entertainment industries looked on. Entertainers Ricky Martin, Seal, and trumpeter Chris Botti performed musical numbers, adding to the richly layered energy of the evening.

It has been said that Tyra Banks has 275 smiles. From the "commercial" smile to the "surprise" smile, and the "coy" smile to the "flirty" smile, Banks learned to transition from one smile to the next in the blink of an eye and look picture-perfect doing so. Since childhood, she has spent much of her life in front of the camera. Banks told interviewer Lynn Hirschberg, "Smiles come naturally to me, but I started thinking of them as an art form at my command. I studied all the time. I looked at magazines, I'd practice in front of the mirror, and I'd ask photographers about the best angles. I can now pull out a smile at will."[1] It was that commitment to her craft—the willingness to research and study and the desire to improve and perfect—that set Tyra Banks apart from other models and helped her rise to the top of the fashion industry.

There was more to Banks than her 275 smiles, however; she was not only a pretty face. Since she was a young girl, Banks had dreamed of working in film and television production. Not only was she interested in being in front of the camera, she also wanted to get behind it. Banks was fascinated by the idea of developing and creating programs. In fact, by the time she appeared in the Tenth Annual Victoria's Secret Fashion Show, Banks was already producing a highly rated reality television program, *America's Next Top Model*. Now Banks wanted to take on daytime by hosting her own television talk show, *The Tyra Banks Show*.

Southern California Girl

Tyra Lynne Banks was born on December 4, 1973, in Inglewood, California, a low-income city southwest of Los Angeles. Tyra's father, Donald (Don), worked as a computer consultant, and her mother, Carolyn London, was a medical photographer at NASA's Jet Propulsion Lab. For a while, Carolyn had been the director of the Medical Media Center at the Hospital of the Good Samaritan. The growing family already had a son, Devin, who would become an air force captain.

Called "Ty Ty Baby" as a child, Tyra grew up in a close, supportive family. As an infant and toddler, Tyra was doted on. Her mother captured many of Tyra's gleeful memories, play dates, holidays, and various facial expressions on camera. On Tyra's Web site, viewers can see photographs from

Tyra's childhood. In addition to photographs of a newborn Tyra and baby pictures of Tyra grinning broadly, there are baby pictures of her with her dad at local parks. In another photo, Tyra is about five, snuggled on Don's lap, both father and daughter sound asleep for a nap.

When Tyra was six, her parents divorced. (Her mother would later marry Clifford Johnson and take his last name, becoming Carolyn London-Johnson.) After the divorce, Tyra lived a one-bedroom apartment in Inglewood with Devin and her mother. Although her father no longer lived with them, he remained a part of Tyra and Devin's lives, and Don and Carolyn stayed cordial to one another. Life, however, became more difficult for the Bankses after the divorce—money was tighter, child care was difficult to come by, and Devin and Tyra had a harder time getting along with each other.

Still, the young family made the best of it. Young Tyra enjoyed dressing up in her mother's clothes and parading around the house in them. She was good at sports and she especially loved basketball. Tyra often attended Los Angeles Lakers games with her dad, even after the divorce. In grade school, Tyra joined the girls' basketball team. Tyra felt confident and happy in her elementary school days. She was often a leader at school, with a ring of friends in her wake. Sometimes Tyra was not as nice as she could have been to other kids who were shyer and less outgoing. Tyra could get sassy and even discriminatory over who she would let play in her circle of friends. The bossiness and dominance Tyra felt in grade school would not last for long, however.

GROWING PAINS

Perhaps because of the family's economic circumstances—needing to keep an eye on the budget because of a single-parent income—Tyra grew up gradually gaining an understanding about money management and the value of saving. Frivolous spending was unheard of in the Banks house. Carolyn taught her children about the importance of living within one's means and saving for the future. Tyra took after her mother. She later told an interviewer, "I'm frugal. I've always been this way. When I was young, my mom would give me my allowance, and I'd peel off a little each week and have some to spare."[1] Even as a little girl, Tyra had a knack for practicality and a budding levelheaded business sense.

A few years after the divorce, Tyra's mother took a second job to help make ends meet. She ran a photography business from her home, London Photography. Her clients were women who wanted glamorous portraits of themselves. Tyra became her mother's helper. Tyra learned a lot from her mother, a skillful and artistic photographer. Carolyn taught Tyra about light and shadow, and how to find the most flattering angles of each client. Carolyn also taught her about the film's development process—including the sequence of steps and how to maximize high-quality shots. Tyra later told an interviewer, "I held [my mom's] light meters and her reflectors. My mom would bring me into the darkroom, which was our back porch, and develop the film. I was fascinated watching the pictures appear with that red light shining. It's so funny that the little assistant holding the lights was a supermodel in the making."[2] Tyra's hands-on work from behind the camera gave her an insider's appreciation for what goes into creating a good photograph. It also was the start of what would become a lifelong passion for photography. Like her mother, Tyra would become an accomplished photographer.

In Tyra's early childhood, her grandmother frequently came to the house. Her grandmother had lung cancer, however, and died at age 50. Tyra was 12 at the time. Tyra's grandmother had been smoking since the age of 13. By the time her grandmother died, the cancer had spread from her lungs to her brain and she no longer knew who she was. Watching her grandmother slowly lose her life in such a difficult manner was hard on Tyra. It was then that Tyra decided she would never become a smoker.

When Tyra was 11 years old, she had a rapid growth spurt. She grew 4 inches (10.2 cm) and lost 30 pounds (13.6 kilograms, or kg) in a span of about three months. The result was a girl so skinny and tall that other girls in her school laughed at her. Tyra's brother, Devin, teased her and called her names relentlessly. She later told a reporter, "At first I was too thin. A little strange, odd-looking. My eyes are too far apart, my chin is narrow, my forehead is very wide."[3] When Tyra went out in public, people stared.

Becoming aware of the cultural preferences for stereo-typical beauty, the once overly confident Tyra suddenly found herself in the position of feeling insecure. Here was a girl who had once dominated the playgrounds and ruled the popular cliques. Now this girl had trouble feeling like she fit in. Tyra frequently cried in her room and felt sad much of the time. She wanted more than anything to be like everyone else—to blend in with ease—but she felt nothing like her peers. Her self-esteem plummeted and she felt far from pretty. She kept to herself, spending much of her time reading books or studying for school—carefully avoiding any interactions with classmates outside her clos-est friends.

Tyra wanted to fix the problem. She wanted people to stop teasing and mocking her about being too tall and skinny. She could not fix the tall, but she *could* try to fill out by putting on weight. In an attempt to gain weight, Tyra tried to eat as many rich, fattening foods as she could. As an adult, she told a reporter from the *Guardian*, "I would come home from school and my brother would make me peanut butter and chocolate shakes. We didn't know about protein, we were just trying to put as much fat in me as possible."[4] Despite all this, Tyra's attempts to gain weight failed. Her gawky appearance did not improve. She remained unusually tall and ultra-skinny. Kids continued to call her names and tease her. Embarrassed, Tyra continued to feel bad about the way she looked. For Tyra, this painfully low period in her life stretched over the next several years.

When Tyra was 12 years old, she tried alcohol for the first (and only) time. She would later tell an interviewer, "I love to eat, but I don't drink. I drank alcohol only once when I was twelve. I had a peach wine cooler down to about the neck. My friend drank hers, drank mine, and then passed out. That was the end of my drinking."[5] Although Tyra didn't feel good about herself at this time in her life, she knew that numbing her feelings with alcohol was not the answer. She had seen the negative effects alcohol had on some of the kids in the neighborhood and at school. She did not like what she saw. Some of these kids had a hard time keeping their grades up. Others dropped out of school altogether. Tyra's parents had impressed upon her how important an education was in helping a person succeed in life.

Preteen Tyra longed to feel less sad and to feel better about the way she looked. She doubled her efforts to place her focus on her school studies and her family. She was trying her best to get through these emotionally charged years of schoolkids' mean-spirited comments on her appearance. So Tyra read even more books, played basketball, watched movies, and continued learning about photography from her mom. Tyra especially enjoyed television. Watching invariably got her imagination going with her own ideas for new types of shows. She would sit for hours and imagine how she would go about bringing her concepts to the screen.

IMMACULATE HEART HIGH SCHOOL

From the ages of 13 to 17, Tyra attended Immaculate Heart High School, located in the Los Feliz section of Los Angeles. At this all-girl Catholic private school, the students all wore matching uniforms. On Tyra's first day of school, something happened that surprised her. Another student approached Tyra and told her that she thought Tyra had the right look to be a model. Tyra was shocked—she was still tall and skinny and awkward. The student insisted, however, that very tall, thin girls were the ones who did well in the fashion industry. She thought Tyra would be a natural on the runway. Tyra did not know what to say. The thought of modeling was totally unexpected—she had thought of herself as the very opposite of what modeling brought to mind: being beautiful.

When Tyra got home from school that afternoon, she told her mother what the classmate had said. Carolyn

IN HER OWN WORDS

As Tyra Banks matured, she began to prioritize elements of her life. She began to see that what may have been important to her in grade school (like being popular) no longer was. Banks was beginning to see that there is more to life than being part of the "in" crowd. As an adult, she told an interviewer:

> I want power. The power to make change. I have never been interested in being "hot" or "cool." I'm not interested in walking down a bunch of red carpets, dating someone famous, being in a big movie. I've done those things, and it never felt right.[7]

soon suggested they take some test pictures. Carolyn had photographed Tyra before, but those photos had been for family enjoyment and fun. Now Carolyn would start taking the kind of pictures Tyra could eventually bring to a modeling agency as part of a portfolio. Tyra liked the idea; she felt comfortable in front of a camera. Over the course of Tyra's high school years, Carolyn photographed and coached Tyra, suggesting angles and poses that best showed off Tyra's strengths. Although Tyra had always felt awkward and clumsy in front of her friends, in front of the camera, she felt relaxed and confident. Tyra found that she could move her body and change positions effortlessly and she had a natural grace and poise. Another change was also taking place: As Tyra matured, she went from being an awkwardly tall, lanky, too-thin girl to being stunningly beautiful.

In 1989 and 1990, when Tyra was 15 and 16 years old and in her junior year of high school, her mother helped her put together her first portfolio of photographs. Then Carolyn took Tyra around to modeling agencies that would find opportunities for her to model—perhaps for catalogues or local advertisements. A disappointing pattern quickly developed: Agencies turned Tyra down—again and again and again. Although the agencies acknowledged Tyra's beauty and grace, they told Tyra that her look was too "ethnic"—clearly meaning too nonwhite. Tyra continued her classes at Immaculate Heart High School and tried not to become discouraged by the repeated modeling rejections. She went on with her schoolwork and continued to practice modeling at home with her mom.

Finally, a well-known agency did accept Tyra—the prestigious Elite Model Management would represent her. Not long after signing, she had her first booking, or modeling job. Tyra would later tell a reporter, "My first modeling job was for a magazine called *Black Collegiate*. I was so excited because there was a little picture of me on the cover, above the title."[6] Tyra had broken into the competitive fashion industry. Most of the early photos taken of Tyra were for department store catalogues and advertisements and for retail stores such as J.C. Penney. Tyra soon fell into a busy

ELITE MODEL MANAGEMENT

Tyra Banks signed with Elite Model Management when she was 17. Elite Model Management is one of the world's most prestigious modeling agencies. John Casablancas and Alain Kittler founded the agency in Paris, France, in 1972. In 1977, the New York branch of the agency opened. Elite Model Management has grown to represent and manage more than 800 models and actors from five continents. Big-name supermodels and actors such as Alyssa Milano, Cindy Crawford, Claudia Schiffer, Gisele Bundchen, Drew Barrymore, Heidi Klum, and Naomi Campbell—along with many others—all modeled with Elite Model Management at some point in their careers.

In an interview with Tom Sykes, Casablancas explained how he helps to make a model, such as Tyra Banks, into a supermodel:

> You have to look into a model—who she really is. She has to have a series of elements put together. She has to be physically attractive, she has to exude elegance, sensuality, movement, and energy. Then she has to have a mental attitude that is interesting or intriguing to the public. You inflame the imagination. Then she becomes not just a pretty face, but a celebrity, and her price becomes 10 times bigger.[8]

Pictured here at right, founder of the Elite Model Management agency John Casablancas attending the Cia Maritima fashion show during Claro Rio Summer at Forte de Copacabana in Rio de Janeiro, Brazil, on November 8, 2008.

routine, dividing her time between school classes, home-work, and modeling.

As high school graduation neared, Tyra needed to think about her future. She had often thought about being a tele-vision or movie producer. She was intrigued with the idea of creating new shows and bringing her creative concepts to the screen. While Tyra found modeling exciting, she was not sure if she would be able to maintain getting jobs. Modeling is a competitive, ever-changing industry where a particular model might be popular one year but out of work the next. Tyra had already found out that her dark skin would sometimes limit her assignments and even keep her from being hired altogether. Also, Tyra knew that modeling was not a long-term career. Models were most successful when they were young. Tyra's mother encouraged her to think about life beyond modeling. Youth would not last forever. If Tyra chose the modeling path, what would she do with herself once she was "too old" for runways and fashion shows?

Tyra started applying to colleges in order to keep her options open. Tyra had always been a good student, and her high grades reflected her efforts. Several schools accepted her, including the University of California, Los Angeles, and the University of Southern California. She was also accepted by Loyola Marymount University (LMU), located in Los Angeles, which became her top prospect. Of the colleges she was accepted by, Tyra decided that LMU was the best fit for her; there, she could study film and television production. The production program at Loyola Marymount would give Tyra training in areas such as cinematography, editing, budgeting, and set design.

Tyra graduated from Immaculate Heart High School in June 1991. The critical time had come. She had to make a commitment about what direction to take her life. Should she try to take her modeling career to the next level— moving out of small-time catalogue work and into the big-name fashion shows—or should she abandon thoughts of modeling and focus on her interest in television and film production by going to college?

High Fashion in Europe

Banks decided on college. She enrolled in Loyola Marymount University and set about preparing herself for the next phase of her life. Then something happened to change that next phase: A high-fashion modeling scout from Paris took notice of Banks. The scout offered Banks the opportunity to model in Paris *haute couture* shows. Haute couture is a French phrase that means "high sewing" or "high fashion." The one-of-a-kind apparel that haute couture designers create can have a great influence on the direction of mainstream fashion trends and styles. Some of the largest haute couture houses today are Giorgio Armani, Chanel, Christian Dior, Christian Lacroix, Givenchy, and Valentino. To be offered work with these elite designers spoke highly of Banks's serious potential in the modeling world. The offer came just weeks before Banks was to begin her freshman year at LMU. If Banks accepted the offer, she would need to postpone or cancel her college plans and move to Europe.

CHANGE OF PLANS

Banks opted to take the opportunity in France. At her mother's suggestion, Banks spent her time learning as much as possible about the fashion industry before her departure. Banks not only wanted to be properly prepared for walking the long runways (something with which she had little experience); she also wanted to know who the top designers were, what the cutting-edge styles were, and more about the history of French fashion. Banks later told a reporter, "My mom explained that I should study the names of the hairdressers, the stylists, the makeup artists, the photographers, the editors, and of course, the designers. I watched videotapes of models walking. My mom said, 'This is not just glamour—it is a business.'"[1] In addition to learning about Paris and its status as a fashion hub, Banks also studied up on other high-fashion European cities, such as Milan, Italy, and London, England. She wanted to be prepared for wherever the job might take her.

So Banks did research. She found that from the Los Angeles Fashion Design Institute's library she could rent videotapes on a variety of fashion topics. Banks watched the videos repeatedly, absorbing as much as she could about fashion's history and present-day workings. In order to study models themselves, Banks also looked for the fashion segments that often appeared on television networks, including MTV and CNN. Banks wanted to learn how they presented themselves, walked, and smiled. Banks would then mimic the fashion models she saw on television. First, Banks would dress up in one of her mother's flowing nightgowns and a pair of her highest-heeled shoes. Then she would practice walking around the house, pretending she was a runway model. She tried different ways of tilting her head, moving her legs, swinging her arms, and striking a pose. Carolyn would watch Banks move, walk, and smile and give advice from the sidelines. Carolyn's feedback and coaching helped Banks develop her own runway style. After long hours of practice, Banks felt ready. She moved to Paris in September 1991, just three months after graduating from high school. Her mother would not be able to join her; she was working two jobs at the time and they could not afford for Carolyn to relocate to Paris. Banks was just 17 years old.

Banks did not completely turn her back on her education; she planned to go to college if the modeling did not work out. She later told an interviewer, "At the beginning [of my career] I gave myself a year to go on auditions and another year to become a supermodel, and if that didn't happen I was going back to school."[2] In the end, however, Banks never needed to attend college.

HITTING THE PARIS RUNWAYS

Banks began her first high-fashion modeling on the brightly lit Parisian runways. At the beginning, Banks was noticeably nervous. Banks would later explain to *People* magazine, "My ankles would shake, and I would bend my knees and stick my lips out."[3] The hours of practice Banks had put in back in California paid off, however. Once she had walked the runway a few times, she gained confidence and her natural abilities began to shine through. She quickly became a top-notch walker. The industry was taking notice; everywhere she went, she was favorably impressing Paris designers. Within a couple of weeks of arriving in Paris, Banks obtained not only a magazine cover, but was also booked for 25 upcoming shows. This feat was not common for a newcomer to couture fashion. The young Banks found herself signing bookings for shows with Giorgio Armani, Karl Lagerfeld for Chanel, Oscar De La Renta, Yves Saint Laurent, and many other big names.

For the next two years, Banks traveled all over Europe for bookings, but primarily in the haute couture hot spots: Paris, Milan, and London. Banks spent hours sitting in hair and makeup, walking runways, and posing for photo shoots. Despite her success, she discovered that modeling frequently left her feeling lonely. In an interview with *Newsweek*, Banks said, "Actresses or singers travel with entourages, with their hair and makeup people and tour managers. Models are alone. Even when you're the biggest supermodel in the world, you're alone."[4]

Thankfully, Banks did make some lasting friendships. One was fellow up-and-coming model Kimora Lee, who was slightly younger than Banks and less comfortable on the runway. It was Banks's nature to reach out and help others, and so she eagerly gave Lee some feedback and advice when Lee approached her. Banks demonstrated how to practice walking and posing. Banks and Lee started to spend more and more time together, becoming good friends. They appeared in many of the same shows. The hectic schedule of modeling left the friends little downtime, so Banks enjoyed someone to talk to and laugh with on the set or backstage.

Despite her rapid success and new friendships, Banks never felt fully comfortable in Paris. She had never lived on her own before and missed her mother. She later told the *New York Times*, "I was successful, but I was intimidated by Paris. It was too beautiful. It was too much for my mass-American self."[5] After two seasons of modeling, Banks struggled with homesickness and the pressures of modeling. One day, feeling low, Banks called her mother from a pay phone and told her she was considering quitting.

Tyra Banks (*right*) and her mother, Carolyn London-Johnson, are photographed backstage before the Victoria's Secret Fashion Show at the 69th Regiment Armory in New York City in 2002.

Carolyn asked her daughter if it would help if she came to Paris and lived with her. Banks now earned enough money that she could support both herself and her mother. Banks thought the arrangement would help. Carolyn quit her jobs in Los Angeles so that she could be with her daughter overseas. Banks felt instantly relieved to have her mother at her side. Carolyn taught her young daughter how to cope with everyday responsibilities and tasks—maneuvering the big city, cooking her own meals, and dealing with the stresses of the fashion industry. In addition to being a good friend, Carolyn acted as her daughter's coach and manager. Together, the women explored the city and continued to study the fashion industry, keeping abreast of which models were in and which had left. Once Carolyn arrived in Paris, she was by Banks's side for every show and photo shoot. Carolyn would be waiting backstage, offering her support and friendship. Having her mother there meant a lot to Banks.

Unlike many young models, Banks was not *only* interested in the actual modeling. She also enjoyed learning the many details and nuances about the industry itself. Back in her hotel room after a day of working a show or a runway, Banks pulled out her notebooks and got to work. She kept careful track of her earnings and expenses. In her notebooks, she logged each job, the date, and her earnings. She made note of the 20 percent that went to her agency. While other models were off at the gym or exploring the city's nightlife, Banks was busy crunching numbers, studying designers' latest fashions, or fine-tuning facial expressions and new stances in the mirror.

Banks's beauty, personality, and strong work ethic helped her land photo assignments with big-name magazines. In 1992, Paolo Roversi photographed her for a spread in *Harper's Bazaar*. In May of the same year, Patrick Demarchelier photographed Banks, Beverly Peele, and Naomi Campbell for an editorial in *Vogue*. Then in August, Banks made the cover of the German *Harper's Bazaar*, and in October, she made the cover of the Spanish *Elle*.

Her speedy rise to the top brought with it a great deal of money. Banks was grateful for the high-paying work, yet she wanted to be able to give back and do something for others. She worked in an industry where beauty and glamour were considered to be everything, yet Banks did not buy into that mindset. She felt that people should love themselves and their bodies, flaws and all. She did not believe in constantly striving for unattainable perfection. Being a young person

Tyra Banks writing in her notebook while lounging in her old bedroom at her mother's house in 1993. Keeping track of her finances in a notebook was a habit she began early in her career.

herself and having lived through teenage years of feeling awkward and ugly and "less than," Banks knew firsthand the anxieties and insecurities young people sometimes felt.

Banks wanted to see insecure, anxious young people take control of their lives, boost their self-esteem, and follow their dreams. She knew, however, that not everyone had the same chances in life. In 1992, she founded the Tyra Banks Scholarship for African-American girls. This scholarship allowed recipients to attend Immaculate Heart High School, the private school Banks had attended. Banks hoped that at least some of these students would be given a chance to better their lives in a way that may not have been possible without the scholarship.

DOWNSIDES TO HIGH FASHION

Banks was realizing that high-fashion modeling had its drawbacks. One drawback was the fact that Banks was not entirely swept away by high fashion itself. She likened the $30,000 gowns she wore on runways to Halloween costumes. Haute couture fashions use the most expensive, luxurious fabrics in the world, such as silk, wool, cashmere, linen, leather, suede, and fur. Haute couture caters to the wealthy and elite socialites. The often outrageous, cutting-edge fashion did not feel entirely real to Banks, who preferred less expensive garments—clothes one might find at boutiques or even at the local mall. As Banks explained to one interviewer, "I could do the job, but I never truly identified with the fashion world."[6] Even to this day, although Banks will dress up for awards shows and Hollywood parties, she does not seek out designer labels. For her everyday wear, Banks has a simpler, more everyday taste in clothes.

In addition, Banks frequently found herself having to deal with prejudice. Just as she had back in Los Angeles, she encountered limited bookings and opportunities in Paris and London because of the color of her skin. She told an interviewer, "[E]very single day of my modeling career, I encountered prejudice. They'd say, 'You can't do this runway show in the winter because you're black.' 'You can't be on the cover.' 'You can't do this campaign.' 'You can't, you can't, you can't.' It never made me bitter, but it did make me hungrier to prove them wrong."[7] When Banks did make a high-fashion magazine cover or an especially elite campaign, she felt she was helping to change and expand the look of couture, which historically had consisted primarily of fair-skinned models.

(continues on page 32)

FASHION PHOTOGRAPHERS

Some of the world's most renowned photographers have photographed Tyra Banks. Some of the many who Banks has posed for include:

Patrick Demarchelier

Demarchelier grew up in a coastal town in France. He moved to Paris, where he started out working in photo labs. Even before he picked up his first camera, Demarchelier says, he was "always taking pictures with my eyes."[8] Today as a leading fashion photographer, he works with clients such as *Harper's Bazaar*, *Marie Claire*, and *Cosmopolitan*. He has photographed many celebrities, including Cindy Crawford, Claudia Schiffer, Johnny Depp, Naomi Campbell, and Princess Diana.

Sebastian Faena

Hailing from Argentina, Faena started earning a living as a fashion photographer before he had finished high school, at the age of 16, and then attended Columbia University in New York. The list of celebrities Faena has photographed includes Faye Dunaway, Jourdan Dunn, Naomi Campbell, Oluchi Onweagba, and Sessilee Lopez.

Russell James

James grew up in Australia. Unsure what career path he wanted to follow, he lived somewhat nomadically in his early life. He did not discover his love of photography until he was 30 years old. James has taken cover shots for numerous magazines, including *Elle*, *Sports Illustrated*, *Vogue*, and *W*. He has also worked with Victoria's Secret and Rolex. James has a love of nature and travels to exotic places, such as the Arctic Circle, the Caribbean, and Australia—using their dramatic settings as backdrop for his models, who include Kate Bosworth, Gisele Bundchen, Halle Berry, Heidi Klum, and Mary J. Blige.

Alexi Lubomirski

Lubomirski was born in England, but moved to Botswana with his mother and stepfather when he was 8 years old. At 11, he developed a love for photography after being given a camera. He attended the University of Brighton in the United Kingdom, where he studied fashion photography. He is now a photographer for *Harper's Bazaar*. In addition to Banks, Lubomirski has photographed other celebrities, including Anja Rubik, Catherine Zeta-Jones, Cate Blanchett, Demi Moore, and Jennifer Lopez.

Steven Meisel

Meisel grew up in the United States. When he was a boy, he opted to draw pictures of women and leaf through fashion magazines over playing with toys. Today, he is a regular photographer for the American and Italian versions of *Vogue* and *W*. Meisel's subjects have included Hilary Swank, Isabella Rossellini, Linda Evangelista, Madonna, and Natalia Vodianova.

Paolo Roversi

Born in Italy, Roversi developed his passion for photography when he went on a family vacation to Spain. He later worked for the Associated Press before opening his own portrait studio in Italy. He then moved to Paris and has stayed there since. In addition to Banks, Roversi has photographed hundreds of big names such as Guinevere van Seenus, Liya Kebede, Natalia Vodianova, Vanessa Paradis, and Vera Wang.

(continued from page 29)

Another drawback to the industry was the rigid requirement of being stick-thin in order to be a successful high-fashion model. Banks told *People* magazine, "I remember one year in Milan, [models] Veronica Webb and Karen Alexander would be going to the gym every single day during the collections. I was like, 'Wow, I want that.' I wish I had that discipline."[9] Banks, however, did not have that discipline. She enjoyed eating. In the two years Banks spent in Europe, her body changed. By 19, she had become much curvier. So curvy, in fact, that Banks's agency had compiled a list of designers who would no longer book Banks because of her weight. These designers thought her chest and her hips were now too large to look appealing in their designs. Banks later told an interviewer, "One day I said to my mom, 'You know what, I'm 123 pounds, 5 feet 10, and my agent told me to lose 10 pounds.' And my mom said, 'That's crazy.' And we went off to get a pizza, in Milan."[10]

At this point, Banks made the decision to get out of haute couture and move into commercial modeling. This idea had been brewing for a while. The detailed charts of earnings and expenses Banks had compiled spoke loudly to her: High-fashion models made less money than commercial models. Having grown up in a single-parent household with money always being a concern and consideration, Banks had a strong desire to become financially secure—with money to spare instead of always feeling pinched. She would later tell the *New York Times*, "I saw that the mass girls with cosmetic and swimsuit calendars made more money than the high-fashion girls. I started looking at Cindy Crawford. She had been a high-fashion girl, and then she segued into being this Americana girl. No black girl ever attempted to be Cindy Crawford. . . . I wanted Cindy's career—I wanted to be the black girl next door."[11]

Breaking
New Ground
in Commercial
Modeling

Banks returned to California after two years in Europe. Although she would return throughout her modeling career for overseas photo shoots and even some runway shows, starting in 1993, Banks turned her focus away from haute couture and toward commercial modeling. Banks was out to prove that she could make it—and become a huge star along the way. She explained to one interviewer, "The beginning of my modeling career was about myself. It was about how many covers can I get, or how many doors can I knock down—because so many people were telling me as a black model I wouldn't be able to accomplish certain things and I wouldn't be successful in the fashion industry—so it was all about me, me, me, me!"[1] Banks felt that the way to success was through commercial modeling.

Commercial modeling catered to a slightly different kind of model—one more fitting of Banks. Haute couture models tend to be incredibly small—in weight, bone structure, and bust. Banks knew that her body type (being as curvy as she was) now lent itself better to swimsuit and lingerie modeling than it did to couture runway modeling. She began posing for *Sports Illustrated*'s annual swimsuit edition. In addition, throughout the 1990s and early 2000s, she continued to appear in and on the covers of major U.S. magazines such as *Cosmopolitan*, *Details*, *Elle*, *Essence*, *Glamour*, *GQ*, *Harper's Bazaar*, *Maxim*, *Shape*, and *Vogue*.

With Banks's success on magazine covers, she was becoming a sought-after model by clothing designers and companies around the world. Throughout the 1990s, Banks had the opportunity to model in major advertisements for such big-name clients as Anna Sui, Calvin Klein, Cover Girl, Dolce & Gabbana, McDonald's, Nike, Tommy Hilfiger, and Victoria's Secret. Even high-fashion Yves Saint Laurent, for whom Banks had walked runways in Paris and Milan, hired Banks to pose for print ads. She also did print ads for companies including Badgley Meschka, Coors Light, Liz Claiborne, Pepsi, Ralph Lauren, and Swatch.

In 1995, Banks signed a five-year contract with cosmetics company Cover Girl as its spokeswoman. (Just two years earlier, in 1993, Lana Ogilvie had become Cover Girl's first African-American spokeswoman—33 years after Cover Girl launched its first cosmetics line.) What Banks had hoped for back in Paris was developing into a reality—she was becoming the black girl-next-door. Like Cindy Crawford, Banks was creating a name for herself as an all-American girl and proving that African-American women can be featured as top supermodels.

CHANGING THE LOOK OF *SPORTS ILLUSTRATED*

In 1996, Banks made history when she made the cover, alongside Argentinean model Valeria Mazza, of *Sports Illustrated*'s swimsuit issue. Until that year, every woman photographed for the cover (since the magazine's first issue in 1964) had been white. Tyra Banks changed that. Mazza and Banks appeared in leopard bikinis with the tag line "South African Adventure" printed alongside. Photographer Walter Iooss Jr. took the *Sports Illustrated* cover shot.

The following year, Banks again appeared on the cover of the swimsuit issue of *Sports Illustrated*—this time alone and clad in a red polka-dot bikini, photographed by renowned photographer Russell James. Once again, Banks had broken ground, becoming the first African American to appear solo on the cover. (The first time Banks had been featured in a spread on the inside of the magazine had been in 1993, a mere four years earlier.)

After her 1997 cover, reporters flooded Banks with questions. They all wanted to ask Banks how it felt to be the first African American on *Sports Illustrated*'s cover. They wanted to know how she so quickly went from being an unknown girl in Inglewood to being a rising star in the modeling world. Banks agreeably spoke to numerous reporters about her feelings surrounding the cover (she felt honored and happy) and her experiences thus far in the fashion industry.

When *BET* magazine approached Banks for an interview, she had already spoken to numerous reporters. So she surprised even herself when she broke down in tears when *BET* began asking her the very same questions. Her tears were not because she felt overwhelmed by the amount of interviewing she had done or because she no longer wanted to talk about her experiences. She broke down because the importance of what she had done suddenly hit her: Banks had brought about a change in the way some people looked at African-American women. Making the cover of *Sports Illustrated* was one small way to show that black women were as beautiful and sexy as white women. Banks now saw it as a huge step for African-American women—in particular, for young African-American girls who wanted to dream big and believe they could go on to do something with their lives. Banks knew that it was not every girl's dream to be a model, but she hoped that she was showing African-American girls with all varieties of dreams that they, too, could be the first in their fields to break down racial walls. Banks hoped that her cover shot gave hope to the next generation.

In addition to booking magazine covers and inside spreads, Banks was being asked back to fashion shows. Although her curvy body was about 20 pounds (9 kg) heavier than most runway models, some designers in high fashion were still seeking out and hiring Tyra Banks. Some of the fashion shows she participated in included collections for Alberta Ferretti, Anna Molinari, Armani, Chanel, Dolce & Gabbana, Donna Karan, Rifat Ozbek, and Yves Saint Laurent.

Tyra Banks was quickly rising to supermodel status. *People* magazine featured her as one of the "50 Most Beautiful People in the World" in 1994 and then again in 1996. Banks was becoming known as the "new Naomi Campbell." Naomi Campbell was, up until that time, the most successful black supermodel. Campbell had been the first black woman to appear on the magazine covers of both French and British *Vogue* and *Time*. Reporters later claimed that Campbell told German-born designer Karl Lagerfeld to ban Banks from Chanel's catwalk. (Lagerfeld designed for Chanel.) The two models became labeled as rivals. Banks told *Essence* writer Deborah Gregory, "It's very sad that the fashion business and press can't accept that there can be more than one reigning black supermodel at a time."[2] Banks had a difficult time coping with the constant comparisons with Campbell.

FROM MODELING TO TELEVISION
TO THE BIG SCREEN

With her busy schedule, Banks did not have much time for dating and romance. Then, however, she met someone who caused her to want to *make* the time. In the spring of 1993, in the midst of her rising modeling career, Banks was introduced to John Singleton, the director of *Boyz N the Hood*, through mutual friends. Banks and Singleton became fast friends, and that friendship quickly developed into a serious romance. The young couple became nearly inseparable.

With a modeling career going strong and the beginning of a new relationship, Banks seemed to have it all. Banks, however, always looking for new opportunities, had not lost her interest in producing television shows and movies. She had also recently developed an interest in acting. So now that she had made a name for herself in modeling, she wanted to tackle television. She auditioned for a recurring role on the NBC sitcom *The Fresh Prince of Bel-Air*, starring Will Smith. Banks got the part. In the fall of 1993, Banks appeared on the show playing Jackie, Will Smith's girlfriend. In 1997, Banks appeared in three episodes of Fox network's *New York Undercover* as a character named Natasha Claybourne. Banks later made guest appearances on other television shows, including *The Hughleys* (as Nicole for one episode in 1999), *Just Shoot Me!* (as herself for two episodes in 1999), *MADtv* (as Katisha for two episodes in 2000), *Felicity* (as Jane Scott for three episodes in 2000), *Soul Food* (as Nina Joseph for one episode in 2001), *All of Us* (as Roni for one episode in 2004), and *American Dreams* (as Carolyn Gill for one episode in 2004).

In 1995, Banks made her film debut in boyfriend John Singleton's movie *Higher Learning*. Singleton wrote and directed the film. Banks worried about people thinking she was getting the part only because she was Singleton's girlfriend, but Singleton assured her that she would have to go

Model Naomi Campbell on the runway wearing a creation by French fashion designer Jean-Paul Gaultier in Paris, France, on October 4, 2008. The rivalry between Campbell and Banks would dominate their relationship for years.

through the audition process just like anyone else. Her previous acting experience on *The Fresh Prince of Bel-Air* helped her prepare for and know what to expect for the audition. She got the role.

NAOMI CAMPBELL

Naomi Campbell is a British-born model of Jamaican and Chinese descent. She was born on May 22, 1970. Her father left her and her mother, Valerie, when Campbell was still an infant. Campbell grew up in a working-class neighborhood of London. She attended high school at the Italia Conti Stage School and went to university at the London Academy for Performing Arts. A fashion executive spotted Campbell while Campbell was window-shopping. Just one year later, a month before her sixteenth birthday, Campbell appeared on the cover of *Elle*.

Campbell also dabbled in the entertainment industry. She appeared briefly on the television sitcom *The Cosby Show*. She also appeared in numerous music videos, including those of George Michael, Michael Jackson, Jay-Z, Macy Gray, and Prince. Campbell released her own album in 1995, called *Baby Woman*. The album did very well in Japan.

Before Banks came on the modeling scene, Campbell had dominated the runways. Both women have been called the world's number one black model. Founder of Elite Model Management John Casablancas told Tom Skykes, "I don't represent [Naomi Campbell] anymore. I repped her originally, and I was the only person ever to fire her. She stayed with us for many years, and she was responsible for a lot of good stuff and a lot of bad stuff. She made me lose Tyra Banks because she didn't feel there was room for her and Tyra at the same agency."[3]

In *Higher Learning*, Banks plays a track runner and college student named Deja. Omar Epps starred in the film; Jennifer Connelly, Ice Cube, and Laurence Fishburne co-starred. Although Fishburne won an Image Award for Outstanding Supporting Actor in a Motion Picture for his part in the movie, *Higher Learning* received mixed reviews. (Banks and Singleton broke up in the spring of 1996, after a three-year relationship.)

In 1999, Banks appeared in the romantic comedy *Love Stinks*, written and directed by Jeff Franklin, the creator of television sitcoms *Full House* and *Hangin' with Mr. Cooper*. French Stewart and Bridgette Wilson starred in the movie; Bill Bellamy and Tyra Banks co-starred. Banks played Bellamy's wife, Holly Garnett. The *New York Times* called it "a one-dimensional comedy that mostly falls flat. It does have a few real laughs, though, and a surprisingly satisfying final plot twist."[4]

OTHER PROJECTS

In addition to posing for photo shoots, taping television shows, and appearing on runways, Banks dedicated some of her time to giving lectures at universities around the country, including Georgetown University, Howard University, Johns Hopkins University, and the University of Houston. During her talks, she spoke about her career, the prejudice she faced as an African-American model, and self-esteem.

Because Banks was frequently traveling, she spent a great deal of time in hotel rooms. As a result, her own home became an important sanctuary—a place to unwind from her hectic schedule and be surrounded by her own things. Her successful career was earning her more money than she had ever had in her life; she decided it was time to purchase a house. In 1995, Banks bought a half-million-dollar house in Hollywood Hills, California. The five-bedroom home overlooked the San Fernando Valley.

Tyra Banks is photographed holding a copy of her book, *Tyra's Beauty Inside & Out*, which was first published in 1998.

When not busy making movies or modeling, Banks could now take part in her favorite relaxing activities, such as watching television and movies or talking on the phone.

With a sanctuary of her own, Banks then decided to try her hand at writing. She wanted to write a self-help book for young women. The book would allow her a format to put forth her beliefs on the importance of building healthy self-esteem. Harper Perennial published *Tyra's Beauty Inside & Out* in 1998. The guide included beauty tips and commentary on fashion, hair, skin care, healthy diet, and cosmetics, but it also addressed self-esteem, sexual concerns, substance abuse, and romance. *Tyra's Beauty Inside & Out* received a favorable review from *School Library Journal*, which called it "a wonderful choice for today's beauty-seeking teens."[5]

In December 1998, Banks's best friend, Kimora Lee (whom she had met in Paris), was getting married to hip-hop mogul Russell Simmons. Lee asked Banks to be her maid of honor. Banks gladly accepted. The small but elaborate wedding took place in Gustavia, on the island of St. Barthelemy in the Caribbean Sea. Banks would later become godmother to the Simmons's daughter, Ming Lee.

A VICTORIA'S SECRET ANGEL

Banks had first modeled for Victoria's Secret when she appeared in television commercials for the lingerie company in 1997. She also started modeling for its store catalogue, and she took part in its annual fashion shows. In 1999, she became one of the original "Angels" who made their debut during the fourth annual fashion show. Other angels included Laetitia Casta, Heidi Klum, Karen Moulder, Daniela Pestova, and Stephanie Seymour. The Victoria's Secret Angels were the most popular Victoria's Secret models who modeled the newest collections. That same year, for the first time ever, Victoria's Secret put the fashion show online. Ed Razek, the chief marketing officer for Victoria's Secret, said of the show, "It was the most visited webcast of any kind in history."[6]

It was while working at Victoria's Secret that Banks took time to learn more about the business side of modeling. She made sure to have a dependable accountant, a savvy business manager, and a knowledgeable attorney to help her keep her financial affairs in order. Banks also depended on her father, Don, to help her manage finances. As Banks became more experienced, she was willing to share her knowledge with younger, less experienced models who wanted to learn more about the economic aspects of the business. Banks felt that talking about her own experiences in the fashion industry could help younger models learn how to become more successful and make it in the industry.

With her warm, open personality and easygoing style, Banks made friends easily. One friend, German-born Heidi Klum (who later became the host of the popular reality television show *Project Runway*), and Banks enjoyed being silly together at shoots for Victoria's Secret. When not in front of the camera, they could joke around and relax.

The undisputed success Banks had with her work at Victoria's Secret officially brought her the title "supermodel." Tyra Banks was the model to book. She was busy with fashion shows, commercials, catalogue modeling, calendar modeling, swimsuit modeling, television shows, and movies. Banks was continuing to prove that African Americans belonged on covers of magazines and as features in catalogues. She was also proving that a woman with a more rounded body could still dominate the fashion industry—both commercial *and* haute couture.

BANKABLE PRODUCTIONS

Banks had created her own production company in 1999. She originally called it Tygirl Incorporated, and then later changed it to Ty Ty Baby. Both names were a tribute to her childhood nickname. But four years later (and four years more mature), Banks decided on a more grown-up name: Bankable Productions. Banks told an interviewer, "I thought Ty Ty Baby was too cute-sounding. I changed it to Bankable because I want to be a real, true producer and produce more than reality TV."[7] Since its name change in 2003, the production company has sought to develop films and television programs that feature strong female characters.

When Banks first opened Tygirl, she hired accountants and specialists to help her better understand the business of running her production company. Although at the start she knew little about spreadsheets and year-end reports, Banks made certain to learn from the best, and she learned quickly. The careful spending habits Banks had developed as a child were still engrained in her. Now, as a businesswoman, she looks for similar traits in the people she hires. Banks told the *New York Times*, "One of the first things I ask when I hire someone who deals with the financials of the company is about their spending habits. How you spend money reveals a lot about you."[8]

IN HER OWN WORDS

Tyra Banks has dreamed of being a film producer since childhood. In an interview with the *Guardian*, she said:

> What I want my strength to be is not just somebody on camera; I want to be strong as a producer, and create new businesses, and ones that empower women, and are not just about me being on camera.[9]

In every new venture Banks takes on, she is careful about assembling a team of people to work with her who are honest and dependable. She wants the same fierce dedication and loyalty from her staff that she feels toward her projects. She told an interviewer, "If you have entrepreneurial dreams, you have to live and breathe it. . . . I worked nonstop. . . . When I hire someone, I have to feel that I connect with them as a person. I'm looking for honest people. I'm looking for loyalty. I'm looking for people who respect people at all levels, from the people who clean the building to the people who own the building. Those are the values that my mother instilled in me."[10]

America's Next Top Model Is Born

How had this awkward, too-skinny teenager blossomed into a confident, self-assured supermodel? Banks told *Ebony* magazine that her success as a model came because, "Believe it or not, I just really know how to pose well. It took me five years to learn what my best angles are."[1] Banks had not only discovered her best angles, she had discovered how to make it and succeed in a primarily white-dominated industry. Tyra Banks was helping to expand the parameters of fashion. Her hard work brought with it more honors: Tyra Banks received the Michael Award (often referred to as the Academy Awards of fashion) for Supermodel of the Year in 1997. *Sports Illustrated* named Tyra Banks Woman of the Year in 2000.

NEW VENTURES

In 1999, Banks obtained an apprenticeship as a youth cor-
respondent on Oprah Winfrey's daytime talk show. For two
seasons, Banks did makeover segments and talked to people.
Her interviewing skills impressed many people. Friendly
and personable, Banks had a natural way of speaking with
people that put them at ease and encouraged them to talk.
She was also exuberant and quick to voice her opinions. She
was good at both listening to those she was interviewing
and also making personal connections and identifying with
certain aspects of their stories.

The work Banks did on *The Oprah Winfrey Show* caught
the eye of Hilary Estey McLoughlin, who was herself working her way up the ladder at Telepictures Productions (of
which she would become president in 2006). McLoughlin
told an interviewer, "[Banks] was really smart and impressive.
Somebody who could command the kind of presence that
you have to have to succeed on television."[2] McLoughlin
even approached Banks about having Banks do her own talk
show. Banks turned her down, at least for the time being.
She told McLoughlin that she wanted to concentrate on her
modeling career. A talk show would have to wait.

Banks continued to look for new ways in which she
could reach out to young African Americans and help them
reach their goals. In 1999, the year Banks turned 26, she
organized a camp called TZone for underprivileged teenage
girls. She wanted a place for young girls to come together
and work on increasing their self-esteem and taking control
of their lives. She saw TZone as a way to empower girls to
do with their lives whatever they may dream.

The weeklong camp was first held in July 2000 near Los
Angeles. The campers spent their days talking about resisting
peer pressure and the importance of embracing positive

(continues on page 50)

OPRAH WINFREY: TALK SHOW QUEEN

Oprah Gail Winfrey was born on January 29, 1954, in Kosciusko, Mississippi. During her childhood, Winfrey lived with her mother, Vernita. Winfrey's parents had never married; her father, Vernon, lived in Nashville, Tennessee. When Winfrey was a teenager, she left Mississippi to live with her father in Tennessee.

In 1971, Winfrey enrolled at Tennessee State University. Five years later, she moved to Baltimore, Maryland, where for eight years she hosted a daytime television program, *People Are Talking.* She then moved to Chicago, Illinois, to host her own morning television show, *A.M. Chicago.*

In 1986, Winfrey appeared on her own talk show, *The Oprah Winfrey Show.* The show quickly gained popularity and a massive viewing audience. Winfrey took ownership of the show and produced it under her own production company, Harpo Productions. (Harpo is Oprah spelled backward.)

Winfrey expanded the format of her successful talk show to share with the viewers her own passions, such as reading. She began a segment on the show called "Oprah's Book Club," during which she brought on authors—many of whom were unknown— to discuss their books. The result of "Oprah's Book Club" was a renewed interest in pleasure reading throughout the country. The worldwide exposure also helped authors (who would otherwise perhaps have remained unknown) soon appear on best-seller lists.

In addition to her talk show, Winfrey has worked in other fields. She owns her own magazine, *O: The Oprah Magazine.* Early in Winfrey's career, she appeared in the film *The Color Purple* (1985). Winfrey pushed for Congress to create a nationwide database of convicted child abusers; President Bill Clinton signed the bill into law in 1994. More recently, Winfrey opened a $40 million academy called the Oprah Winfrey Leadership Academy for Girls in South Africa. The academy

Talk show host and media mogul Oprah Winfrey at the Emmy Awards in Los Angeles on September 21, 2008. Banks's experience as an intern on Winfrey's talk show proved to be enormously beneficial for her.

offers 450 underprivileged students food, uniforms, textbooks, and free tuition. Winfrey also campaigned for Democratic presidential hopeful Barack Obama in December 2007.

(continued from page 47)

values. The campers spent their nights at the campsite, bonding and sharing their individual stories. Banks herself lived with and talked with the campers. She asked campers to call her by her nickname, BBQ, after her love of barbecued food. She wanted the girls to feel comfortable with her and not feel intimidated by her celebrity status.

Banks has always felt it is important to let young girls know how deceptive the fashion industry is. She wants them to understand that she, herself, has flaws, just like everyone else—including other supermodels. Banks told *Jet*, "[The fashion industry is] an industry that projects one image as beautiful, and no one really looks like that! That's why it's so important to show young women the retouching, styling, and makeup tricks they use to make models look perfect. In fact, it's irresponsible not to show that stuff. I want to empower women to embrace their flaws—showing mine is just a part of that."[3] The honesty and frankness with which Banks spoke to the campers helped them to feel safe and to develop a strong connection with her.

In 2000, Banks appeared in three movies, none of which received rave reviews. Gina Prince-Bythewood wrote and directed *Love & Basketball*. Roger Ebert said of it, "[*Love & Basketball* is] a thoughtful and touching story about two affluent black kids, a boy and a girl, who grow up loving each other, and the game."[4] Banks also appeared in Disney's made-for-television movie *Life-Size*, written and directed by Mark Rosman. Banks, Lindsay Lohan, and Jere Burns starred in the film. Banks plays Eve, a doll brought to life by a young Lohan. Banks also performed a song called "Be a Star" for the film. The final movie, *Coyote Ugly*, was directed by David McNally and written by Gina Wendkos. Piper Perabo and Adam Garcia star in the film. Banks plays a character named Zoe. Like *Love & Basketball*, *Life-Size* and *Coyote Ugly* received poor reviews from critics.

A couple of years later, in 2002, Banks appeared in a horror movie, *Halloween: Resurrection*, in which she played Nora Winston. *Halloween: Resurrection* was a box-office flop. The *Los Angeles Times* noted that "there's not nearly enough scares, or humor, to make *Halloween: Resurrection* worthwhile."[5]

TRAGEDY STRIKES

On the morning of September 11, 2001, tragedy struck in the United States. Osama bin Laden had ordered members of the al Qaeda terrorist organization to attack the World Trade Center in New York City and the Pentagon outside Washington, D.C. The terrorists hijacked four commercial U.S. airplanes and crashed the first plane into the north tower of the World Trade Center and the second into the south tower. The third plane crashed into the Pentagon, and the fourth plane crashed in a Pennsylvania field after some of the passengers tried to stop the hijackers. The people aboard all four planes died instantly, and almost 3,000 people died as a result of the destruction that the airplanes caused. The events of 9/11 would affect the lives of the American people for years to come. Businesses crumbled. People lost their jobs and their homes. Fires burned for 99 days after the attacks. The cost to clean up the disasters totaled $600 million.

Banks had been in New York on the day of the disaster. Years later, she would remember that morning, saying, "I was in New York City and I was lying in bed and I turned on the TV and what I saw was unimaginable . . . and then I looked out the window and I was like, 'This is real.' Everybody worked together that day and during that time. It didn't matter what race you were, what sex you were, everybody worked together."[6]

CREATING *AMERICA'S NEXT TOP MODEL*

In 2002, Banks developed the concept that would become the blockbuster reality TV show *America's Next Top Model*.

Here, Banks is photographed with her TZone Youth Camp at the Scripps College in Claremont, California, on July 21, 2005.

The idea came to her one morning while she was preparing tea in her kitchen. Right away, she knew she had a potential hit. Prior to this idea, Banks had approached her agent with other premises for television shows, but each time, her ideas had been rejected. Banks felt confident about this one: She wanted to host a reality show in which contestants competed against each other to win a modeling contract. Yet when Banks approached her agent, she was met with the same knee-jerk response: Her agent rejected it.

Banks did not want to let go of this idea. She decided to seek a second opinion. She spoke to a friend and writer, Kenya Barris, who liked the concept and helped Banks set up a meeting with reality television producer Ken Mok. Mok, who produced the reality television show *Making the Band*, was immediately impressed and intrigued. He did not know what to expect from Banks, however, until he met her. Then he quickly decided she was a person with whom he could work easily. He told an interviewer, "All I knew about Tyra was her *Sports Illustrated* swimsuit cover and that, at the time, she had dated the basketball star Chris Webber. I'm more of a football guy than a model guy, and I thought, 'This is going to be a vanity project where I will do all the work and she will get an executive-producer credit.' Five minutes into the conversation, I realized that she was very driven and keenly smart. I'm an incredibly ambitious person, but Tyra makes me look lazy."[7]

After Mok was sold on the idea and on Banks's abilities as a co-producer, he and Banks took the concept to CBS. They liked the idea as well and thought it would be a good fit for their sister network, UPN. (UPN later combined with WB and became the CW network.) UPN also liked the premise and committed to launching the show. *America's Next Top Model* was born.

The basic format of *America's Next Top Model* has remained the same for each cycle, or season. Ten to 14 girls (the number varies from season to season) are thrown together in an apartment where the girls face each other's differing opinions, beliefs, and personalities. Tempers flare, jealousies surface, and friendships form.

Contestants are filmed 24/7 as they deal with living together while competing, going on assignments, and taking part in photo shoots. The main photo challenge of each episode is often something extreme—posing next to a burning car, wearing raw meat as part of their garment, or portraying natural disasters (blackout, sandstorm). During this photo shoot, Canadian-born Jay Manuel, who acts as the creative director and producer, explains the task to the models, oversees direction, and offers his feedback.

At the end of each episode, contestants are brought to a judging room. The judges for Cycle 1, along with Banks, were Janice Dickinson, Kimora Lee Simmons, and fashion editor and stylist Beau Quillian. In the judging room, Banks and her team of judges look at each girl's best photo from the main photo shoot of the episode and speak briefly with each contestant. Then the girls are sent away while the judges deliberate, evaluating the models' strengths and weaknesses. The judges then decide which contestant is the weakest and must leave the show.

After bringing the contestants back in, Banks calls out the names of the contestants who will continue competing, in order of how well they have done that week, the strongest competitor being revealed first. As Banks says each name, she hands that model her best photograph. The bottom two contestants are then asked to step forward. In a low, somber voice, Banks dramatically explains to each model why the judges felt they were the weakest models that week. Banks then announces the name of the last model safe from that week's elimination. The name that she does not call is asked to return to the apartment, pack her bags, and leave the show. Before that contestant leaves, however, Banks gives her a hug and offers her support and constructive suggestions for her future.

America's Next Top Model is an ideal platform to showcase Banks's huge personality. At times, she sympathizes with the contestants' struggles and offers words of encouragement. Other times, she critiques the women bluntly with seemingly little care. Banks does not take kindly to contestants who seem to give up. She wants women with strong work ethics who are willing to put in the needed practice and study time. She tells one interviewer, "We're in a day and age when these kids want instant success, and they don't want to work for it. I feel tough love prepares these girls."[8]

Banks, realizing that American television audiences *want* to watch drama and excitement, adds, "I've got to sell a TV show."[9] Sell, Banks does. When Banks is on-screen, she frequently engages in theatrical behavior—dressing up in wild costumes, talking in strange accents, or breaking into dramatic song or dance.

During one episode each season, the girls are given a makeover, emphasizing new hairstyles that help elevate them from pretty girls to models. Each season also includes an international destination, where the show takes the contestants to another country to compete. Cycle 1's international destination was Paris, France, the city where Tyra launched her career.

CYCLE 1

America's Next Top Model first aired in May 2003. Its debut took place when other reality TV shows, including CBS's *Survivor*, MTV's *Real World*, and Fox's *American Idol*, were extremely popular. In the first season of *America's Next Top Model*, 10 female contestants, ages 18 to 26, competed to become the "top model." The winner, announced in the last episode, received a modeling contract with Wilhelmina Models, a contract with Revlon cosmetics, and a layout in *Marie Claire*.

The first season had its share of rough patches. The troubles began with casting. It was difficult to draw interested contestants for this never-before-seen reality show. In addition, there were limited money and resources available. Banks told an interviewer, "The clothes the girls wore in the poster for the first season came from my closet because we couldn't afford a stylist. I had to carry those clothes in a trash bag on the airplane because I was scared to check it. I thought, if they're lost, there are no clothes for the shoot."[10]

Despite these difficulties, Cycle 1 got under way with 10 girls competing. In order of elimination, they were: Tessa Carlson, Katie Cleary, Nicole Panattoni, Ebony Haith, Giselle Samson, Kesse Wallace, Robin Manning, and Elyse Sewell. Shannon Stewart was the runner-up, and Adrianne Curry, from Joliet, Illinois, became the Cycle 1 winner. America had its first "top model." UPN president Dawn Ostroff said of the process, "The core of *America's Next Top Model* is about who [the contestants] are inside and breaking down all the barriers for these girls so they can get to know their real selves and let the real them come out and blossom."[11]

Curry's win on the show brought her bookings for modeling jobs from Macy's, and she appeared in magazines and television commercials. She also landed a role on another reality series, *Surreal Life*, on VH1. Here, she met and fell in love with co-star Christopher Knight, who had played Peter Brady on the classic television show *The Brady Bunch*. Knight and Curry began a spin-off to *The Brady Bunch*, called *My Fair Brady*, premiering in 2005. It ran for three seasons; in the second season, Knight and Curry get married.

AMERICA'S NEXT TOP MODEL TAKES OFF

Initially, there was little promotion for *America's Next Top Model*. Despite this, the show quickly became a success. In the eyes of Telepictures then-president, James Paratore, this feat said a lot about Banks. He told an interviewer, "[The show's success despite little promotion] spoke volumes to me about this connection [Tyra Banks] had with women. It was a lot deeper than just being a model."[15] In the age range of 18- to 34-year-olds, 43 percent of them had never before watched programs on UPN. Now, after the launch of *America's Next Top Model*, UPN was drawing huge numbers of new viewers from this demographic. Banks, who owns 25 percent of the show, profited handsomely from its success.

In Cycle 2, which first aired in January 2004, 12 contestants competed. The show was becoming so popular that it began rebroadcasts of the show the day after the original airing, giving UPN even higher ratings. This season, the girls flew to Italy for their international destination. There were also new judges. Beau Quillian was replaced with Eric

DID YOU KNOW?

Banks is continually looking for new ventures. With *America's Next Top Model* established and successful, she was ready to branch out again. Banks had long wanted to be a singer. She told *Jet*, "[Music] is something I grew up with. My mom has a beautiful voice. I heard that every day."[12] Banks had trained with vocal coaches for six years to improve her voice in hopes of breaking into the music industry.

She hired music manager Benny Medina, who has worked with Mariah Carey and Jennifer Lopez, and producer Rodney Jerkins, who has worked with Whitney Houston and Mary J. Blige. Jerkins appreciated Banks's exceptional work ethic and dedication. He told *Jet*, "[Tyra Banks] has what it takes to pull it off. She had a hungriness to want to be in the studio all the time. Some people want to be divas in the studio and work for three or four hours. You had to tell Tyra to stop or she will keep you going. She's a consummate professional."[13]

Medina and Jerkins helped Banks to release a single, "Shake Ya Body." Banks used her own money to finance a music video, which debuted on *America's Next Top Model*, Cycle 2. It became the most downloaded song on UPN's Web site. Still, the song did not gain momentum with the public. Of her failed attempt at a singing career, Banks notes, "Just because you have access to something doesn't mean it's right for you."[14]

Nicholson, and Nigel Barker took the place of Kimora Lee Simmons. Nicholson was a former editor of *Jane*. British-born Barker was a model in England and became a photographer.

The contestants, in order of elimination, were Anna Bradfield, Bethany Harrison, Heather Blumberg, Jenascia Chakos, Xiomara Frans, Catie Anderson, Sara Racey-Tabrizi, Camille McDonald, April Wilkner, and Shandi Sullivan. Mercedes Scelba-Shorte was the Cycle 2 runner-up, and Yoanna House, a 24-year-old nanny from Jacksonville, Florida, was the Cycle 2 winner. House won a contract with IMG Models, an ad campaign with Sephora cosmetics, and a spread in *Jane* magazine.

Cameras continued to roll after Cycle 2 ended. In May, *America's Next Top Model: The Runway Ahead* aired on television. The special followed House as she was introduced to runways, designers, and fellow professional models. It also followed the other contestants as they returned to their lives after the show. Viewers saw how the girls' lives had changed as a result of the competition.

In Cycle 3, which began airing in September 2004, Banks increased the number of contestants to 14. It became the highest-rated season yet. UPN president Dawn Ostroff explained, "The success of ["America's Next Top Model"] has been tremendous for UPN. Everything in the show—including the characters, the drama, the catfights, the triumphs, and the storytelling—all come together to make the show a ratings success."[16]

The girls' international destination for Cycle 3 was Japan. Once again, there was a slight change in the makeup of judges. Joining Banks, Barker, and Dickinson was Nolé Marin, a fashion icon who works as a celebrity stylist. His list of celebrity clients includes Alicia Keyes, Claudia Schiffer, Heidi Klum, Kanye West, Kimora Lee Simmons, Ricky Martin, Tommy Hilfiger, and Tyra Banks. In order of elimination, the contestants were Magdalena Rivas, Leah Darrow, Julie Titus, Kristi Grommet, Jennipher Frost, Kelle Jacob, Cassie Grisham, Toccara Jones, Nicole Borud, Norelle Van Herk, Ann Markley, and Amanda Swafford.

Yaya Da Costa was the Cycle 3 runner-up, and Eva Pigford (nicknamed "Eva the Diva" on the show) became the first African American to win the title of "America's Next Top Model." Like Banks, Pigford was not popular in high school. She later told interviewer Andrea Tuccillo, "I wasn't that cool girl in high school. I wasn't the one in the cliques. I had three brothers, I had long hair I had nothing to do with, I was skinny, I ran track, I wasn't a cheerleader."[17] Pigford's win brought her a contract with Cover Girl, a spread in *Elle*, and representation by Ford Models. After Pigford appeared in numerous magazines, she landed a role on *The Young and the Restless*.

Pigford talked to one interviewer about what it was like working with Tyra Banks on *America's Next Top Model* and how their relationship had developed since the end of the show. Pigford said, "Just because you're a star and you're great at what you do doesn't mean that you can necessarily produce someone else, but Tyra does a very good job. During filming, we weren't really allowed to cultivate a relationship with Tyra because she was one of the judges, and so she and I weren't as close then, but now we definitely have a relationship and I speak to her a lot. When I have an issue or I'm going to meet with a client for a casting, I'll call her for advice about what to wear and she gives me talking points."[18]

By Cycle 4, *America's Next Top Model* had become a staple on the reality television scene. Ostroff admitted, "I just didn't think Tyra had that talent. I knew she had a great idea, but I didn't know that she would be an incredible executive producer, where she would have the ability to edit, create different segments, and where she would be so great in casting."[19] Cycle 4 began in March 2005 with 14 contestants. The same judges from Cycle 3 returned for Cycle 4. The contestants flew to South Africa for their international destination. Kahlen Rondot was the Cycle 4 runner-up, and Naima Mora was the Cycle 4 winner. As in Cycle 3, Mora won a contract with Cover Girl, a spread in *Elle*, and representation by Ford Models.

The
Tyra Banks
Show

In 2005, Banks turned her TZone camp into a public charity called the Tyra Banks TZone Foundation. This nonprofit organization honors the camp's origins and reaches a national support group to which it offers grants. Its Web site notes that it "identifies and provides resources to a network of community nonprofits recognized for their impact on girls and young women, empowering them to take control of their lives and go after their dreams—whether through community activism, dance, filmmaking, leadership, sports, writing, or as young entrepreneurs—however they choose to create their best futures."[1] In 2008, TZone awarded $10,000 each to four nonprofit organizations that aim to better the lives of young women.

The first was the Sadie Nash Leadership Project of Manhattan, which helps teach young women critical-thinking skills while increasing self-esteem and improving self-image. The second was the Ifetayo Cultural Arts organization based in Brooklyn, New York, which hosts a Sisterhood Rites of Passage program where young adult women learn how to become strong leaders. The third was the Lower East Side Girls Club of New York, aimed at girls and young women between the ages of 8 and 25. This program encourages positive actions and teaches critical-thinking skills. The final organization was the GirlSpeak program of the Young Chicago Authors, which gives high school girls an opportunity to discuss, write, and perform ideas about women's issues.

Giving grants to programs such as these brings hope and change to women's lives. The executive director of TZone, Marian Gryzlo, said, "TZone encourages girls and young women to become driving forces in their own lives. We want girls to be leaders, not followers, in control, not out of control, empowered, not powerless, about creating their best futures and going after their dreams."[2] Banks, Gryzlo, and the other members of the TZone staff seek organizations that will promote, teach, and encourage these values.

Banks continues to be involved in the foundation's direction and oversees grant approvals and activities. She feels a strong connection with young women and wants to see them become strong forces, not shying away: "TZone is not a place—it is a commitment to empower girls to be fierce, focused, and in control of their futures."[3] In 2008, Banks would move her TZone Foundation from California to New York. In an interview with the *New York Times*, Banks said, "I think I was put on this earth to instill self-esteem in young girls."[4]

DAYTIME TALK

By 2005, Banks had been modeling professionally for 15 years. She had graced the covers of magazines, glided down runways, and smiled to sell products. Now, however, Tyra Banks was ready for yet another change: She announced to the world that she was officially retiring from modeling. She would do one more runway show at the end of the year—the Tenth Annual Victoria's Secret Fashion Show. Then she would stop booking runway shows. Banks was ready to take on a new challenge—daytime talk television.

When Hilary Estey McLoughlin approached Banks about doing a talk show back when she had been apprenticing on *The Oprah Winfrey Show*, Banks had declined. Now, however, Banks was ready to make a commitment to developing her own talk show. She contacted McLoughlin, who was thrilled and set to work drawing up a deal. Tyra Banks launched her talk show in 2005. As she does with *America's Next Top Model*, Banks owns part of her talk show. She co-owns the show with her firm, Bankable Productions, and Telepictures. Banks enjoys taking part in the behind-the-scenes activities as well as being the show's host. She told an interviewer, "I love coming up with topics and my producers pitching me ideas and shaping it and dealing with budgets."[5]

The Tyra Banks Show would be filmed in Los Angeles, in the traditional one-hour talk-show format. Banks keeps an unusually sparse set, though her exuberant personality more than makes up for it. She tapes 170 episodes a year. From August to December 2005, Banks put in 12-hour days, 7 days a week, splitting her time among *America's Next Top Model* (then in Cycle 5), *The Tyra Banks Show*, and preparing for her final Victoria's Secret Fashion Show. During this time, Banks was often getting by on only three or four hours of sleep at night.

The Tyra Banks Show quickly grew in popularity—especially among young women. The show draws some 2.2 million viewers between the ages of 18 to 34 each week. About 36 percent of Banks's audience is younger than 35. (*The Oprah Winfrey Show* draws only half that in the same age group.) Banks told the *New York Times*, "I have always felt 19. It's a little embarrassing, but I can easily put myself in the mind of a teenager. And I know what they think about, how they feel. Teenagers don't like when you preach to them, but if you surround the medicine with a little bit of candy, they'll listen. And then they'll learn something."[6] Not only does Banks reach her audience members easily, she connects with her staff and sponsors. Banks makes a point of meeting and greeting every potential advertiser of her talk show. She even does much of the selling herself.

TYRA BANKS: TALK SHOW HOST

Banks tries to keep her show feeling candid and edgy. She believes in no rehearsals—she likes the show to have a slightly improvised look (although, in reality, they are carefully scripted). Nor does Banks use a teleprompter. She is not afraid of making mistakes on the air. In fact, she has said, "We are beautiful with our imperfections on 'The Tyra Show.'"[7] Banks believes everyone has flaws and makes mistakes, and she wants more people to be accepting of that fact.

Banks uses her flamboyant personality to help make her point. She will appear on the show wearing no makeup to prove that beauty is not all about outer beauty—it is about inner beauty, too. She will be loud and brash to prove prim and proper is not "better." Banks can also be serious when she needs to be. She knows how to entertain, how to have fun, how to listen, how to teach, and how to empathize. Banks does not come across as a standoffish, elite supermodel-turned-talk-show-host; she makes herself accessible to everyday people.

What makes *The Tyra Banks Show* so popular is Banks's easygoing, "girlfriend" attitude, coupled with the wide range of topics she covers. She handles typical adolescent and young adult concerns about weight gain, weight loss, beauty tips, healthy eating, and exercise, and also tackles more difficult and controversial topics such as teenage pregnancies and marriages, homelessness, divorce, sexual identity, and race. She told the *New York Times*, "I'm not afraid to talk about race. We did a show where a focus group was asked what came to mind when they heard names like Ashleigh or Deedrica and José. We didn't tell them to discuss race, but all these racial stereotypes came out. They thought Ashleigh was pretty and blond. Deedrica was black and José would 'steal my momma's car.' When we revealed to them that Deedrica was a white child and Ashleigh was a black child, the audience got so angry."[8] Banks stirs emotions. She gets her audience and viewers thinking. She raises questions, sparks debate, and shares personal stories. As a host—just as she was as a model—Tyra Banks is a natural.

As often as she can, Banks uses her show to build self-esteem in young people. One way she does this is to deglamorize herself and represent herself as an average person with problems and worries similar to mainstream Americans. She willingly shows before-and-after photos of herself to let people see that editors can trim inches from models' thighs and waists in order to "improve" a photograph. She told *Jet*, "As someone who portrays an unattainable image but was also teased relentlessly growing up, I understand and can relate to many young women's insecurities. I feel that if I can reach out to someone and touch just one person through my talk show, I have done my part. I feel it is my responsibility to let women of all ages know that true beauty comes from within; it's not what you see in magazines."9

Banks is quick to share stories about the long hours spent getting made up with makeup, hair extensions, and tummy-cinching clothing accessories in order to give the *appearance* of perfection when she steps in front of a camera. Banks uses her show to drive home that nobody is perfect—not even supermodels. She knows from experience that modeling and advertising are all about putting forth illusions to the public—modeling gives an illusion of ultimate beauty and advertising gives an illusion of an ideal product. Yet, just as the audience is deceived in a magic show, what the public sees is not the whole truth. By sharing this knowledge with her viewers, Banks hopes young people see that magazines and advertisements are portraying unrealistic ideals of women's bodies. Banks wants young people to find the individual inner and outer beauty they each have and use it to build strength and confidence.

MODELS ON *THE TYRA BANKS SHOW*

In addition, Banks brings a wide range of special guests on her show. She interviews actors, authors, models, politicians, and even family members—in fact, both of her parents have appeared on her show. Banks also frequently brings contestants from *America's Next Top Model* on her talk show. Almost 90 percent of the *America's Next Top Model* audience also watches *The Tyra Banks Show*, so fans can look forward to learning more about their favorite contestants on the talk show.

From Cycle 4, Banks brought on winner Naima Mora as well as her twin sister, Nia, who is a New York photographer. Naima and Nia had been having trouble with their relationship since Naima's win on *America's Next Top Model*. Even prior to the win, the sisters had been abusing

The panel of judges for Cycle 5 of *America's Next Top Model*. Pictured from left to right are former British fashion model Twiggy, runway expert J. Alexander, creator and executive producer Tyra Banks, and photographer Nigel Barker.

alcohol and drugs as a way of dealing with the stress in their lives—and, in Nia's case, also for dealing with depression. Since the win, Nia's drug and alcohol abuse had continued. Naima, though not using drugs, was still using alcohol as a way to relieve stress. On the show, Naima revealed feeling pressure to book shows while still making time for Nia as she had before winning *America's Next Top Model*. The demands of Naima's newly hectic schedule, however, were making that impossible. Nia was feeling Naima's stress and ultimately falling into a deeper depression. Both sisters felt a loss of control over their lives.

Banks, wanting to help them both be safe and strong and take control of their lives once again, introduced them to Dr. Keith Ablow, who spoke to each of the sisters separately and then together about their struggles. Portions of the one-on-one meetings with the sisters were aired on *The Tyra Banks Show*. Also during the episode, Ablow, along with Tyra, talked to Naima and Nia in front of the audience. Ablow helped the women to identify their feelings and gave them direction in turning their lives around.

In another heart-to-heart episode about repairing relationships, Banks brought on supermodel Naomi Campbell. For their entire modeling careers, Campbell and Banks had been pegged as rivals. Banks wanted to clear the air between them, once and for all. Banks began the interview talking about how, for her, the feud between herself and Campbell had been frustrating and damaging. She admitted to still feeling a little scared of Campbell. Banks reminisced about the icy photo shoots with Campbell at which the tension was thick and uncomfortable. They would be posing together, but never once talking or interacting personally. Banks told Campbell that their rivalry had affected her and hurt so much that it had sometimes made her want to give up on modeling altogether. Before Banks's mother had joined her in Paris, Banks felt especially alone. Banks was not sure Campbell was hearing her when Campbell remarked during the interview that she felt the media had overblown the feud.

This first part of the interview was taped and aired on television, but it was done without an audience; Banks had not wanted live witnesses there when she faced Campbell for the first time after 14 years. Once they had spoken with each other alone, however, Banks brought the audience in and did the remaining portion of the show with the audience. When introduced during that segment, Campbell began by saying that she wanted to tell Banks how proud she was of Banks's career and what Banks had done for the African-American community. Banks responded by saying how much that meant to her and that it made her feel like Campbell was owning up to her part of the rivalry. Banks and Campbell both became emotional; with the tears came a long-overdue hug.

The two supermodels have remained friendly since the show. Banks told one interviewer, "I had dinner with [Campbell] maybe a few months ago, and it's actually really refreshing to have that type of relationship with her. Before, I was kind of scared of her. But after she came on my show, it's been great. I see her on the street in New York and I yell her name and she calls me over. I really do think it's genuine."[10] Banks was relieved to have put the long rivalry to rest and to feel she could move on with her life.

TRAGEDY STRIKES THE GULF COAST

On August 25, 2005, Hurricane Katrina hit just north of Miami, Florida. Four days later, the eye of the hurricane swept across southeastern Louisiana early in the morning. Within a few hours, much of the levee system in New Orleans collapsed, causing Lake Pontchartrain and the Mississippi River to flood nearly the entire city. The hurricane damaged coastal regions of Louisiana, Mississippi, and Alabama. More than 1,800 people died as a result of the hurricane. It caused about $200 billion in damage. More than a million people were displaced. Thousands of these were bused to neighboring states.

Tyra Banks wanted to help. Later that year, in December, she announced on her talk show an exclusive release of neo-soul singer India.Arie's song "What About the Child" to raise funds for children affected by Hurricane Katrina. Banks had first worked with India.Arie to write the theme song for *The Tyra Banks Show*. That song, called "Just for Today," had been highly successful.

Banks invited India.Arie to perform "What About the Child" live on her talk show. India.Arie did perform at the talk show, though the performance was not played on the air. Banks established a partnership with iAmplify to make the song available for download for one dollar—the benefits going directly to aid affected children. Television viewers could also give larger donations to the cause by buying VIP tickets to see a taping of *The Tyra Banks Show*. These donators would also be acknowledged in the show's credits. Another way viewers could donate was to purchase T-shirts with lyrics from the show's theme song, "Just for Today." The T-shirts were available on the show's Web site. All of the money raised from the show, the purchase of India.Arie's song, and the purchase of the T-shirts went to UNICEF's Hurricane Katrina Fund.

AMERICA'S NEXT TOP MODEL CYCLES 5 THROUGH 7

Simultaneous with her work on her talk show, Banks continued taping new episodes of *America's Next Top Model*. In Cycle 5, which first aired in September 2005, two new judges joined Banks and Barker: Twiggy and J. Alexander. In the 1960s, Twiggy became the world's first teenage supermodel when she was 17 years old. In addition to modeling, Twiggy has recorded albums, led a successful career as a stage, television, and film actress, and designed a clothing line. J. Alexander, known as "Miss J" on *America's Next Top Model*, started out as a runway model for Jean-Paul Gaultier. Now he coaches runway models for top designers.

Nik Pace became the Cycle 5 runner-up and Nicole Linkletter was the Cycle 5 winner. There were 13 cast members in this cycle, and contestants traveled to the United Kingdom for their international destination. The prizes, once again, were a Ford Models contract, a spread in *Elle*, and a contract with Cover Girl. Linkletter also won a magazine cover with *Elle Girl*.

In Cycle 6, the 13 contestants traveled to Thailand toward the end of the season. The show began in March 2006. Joanie Dodds was the Cycle 6 runner-up, and Danielle

THE TYRA BANKS SHOW IN THE NEWS

According to Tyra Banks, her talk show has a dual mission: to entertain but also to get people talking and thinking about issues they may not have dealt with before. Within the context of the show's public forum, Banks has been able to educate and familiarize her audience and television viewers about the lesbian, gay, bisexual, and transgender (LGBT) community. In 2008, Banks dedicated numerous shows pertaining to the LGBT community, including "Transgender Triumphs," which highlighted specific transgender stories; "Don't Ruin My Gay Wedding," which promoted marriage equality; and "Gays in the Ghetto," which alerted viewers to the gay bashing and discrimination homosexuals face on a daily basis.

Banks's frank presentations of the complex issues faced by the LGBT community encourage her viewers to face their own underlying bias against people with different lifestyles. Because of her work to increase the visibility and understanding of the lesbian, gay, bisexual, and transgender community through her talk show, Banks was honored in 2009 at the twentieth annual Gay and Lesbian Alliance Against Defamation (GLAAD) Media Awards with an Excellence in Media Award. GLAAD president Neil Giuliano said of Banks and fellow special honoree Suze Orman, "Tyra Banks and Suze Orman have used their positions of power within the media to become strong advocates on behalf of the LGBT community. They are changing hearts and minds, opening people's eyes to our common humanity, and it is our privilege to honor them."[11]

Evans was the Cycle 6 winner. Twenty-year-old Evans won a Ford Models contract, a spread in *Elle*, and a contract with Cover Girl. Cycle 7, beginning September 2006, was the first season to air on the newly formed CW network. Melrose Bickerstaff was the Cycle 7 runner-up, and photographer-turned-model CariDee English was the Cycle 7 winner. Contestants traveled to Spain for their international destination. Beginning with Cycle 7 (and through Cycle 11), the winners received management and representation by Elite Model Management, a six-page spread in *Seventeen* magazine, and a $100,000 contract with Cover Girl.

Cycle 7 winner English has battled psoriasis (severely dry skin) for the majority of her life. At one point, psoriasis covered 70 percent of her body. She began taking a medication that helped control the psoriasis; unfortunately, there is no medication available that cures it. In 2007, English traveled to Washington to speak on behalf of the National Psoriasis Foundation in support of the Psoriasis and Psoriatic Arthritis Research, Cure, and Care Act. This

IN HER OWN WORDS

Tyra Banks knows what it takes for someone to overcome obstacles that stand in the way of his or her dreams. In an interview, Banks recalled:

> When I was a model, my biggest obstacle was that I was black and curvy. When I went into producing, my biggest obstacle was that I was a model. But, as I say to the girls on *Top Model*, anybody who is at the top of anything has taken risks and withstood criticism and hardship.[12]

bill marked the first comprehensive psoriasis legislation introduced by Congress.

POLITICIANS ON *THE TYRA BANKS SHOW*

In 2008, Banks invited some of the presidential candidate hopefuls to her show. In the fall of 2007, Banks hosted an especially noteworthy episode of her talk show: She interviewed Democratic presidential candidate Barack Obama. Banks had first met Obama at Oprah Winfrey's Legends Ball in 2005. Obama's appearance on *The Tyra Banks Show* was his first hour-long interview since he had announced his candidacy.

Banks and Obama discussed wide-ranging topics: the prejudices Obama faced over the course of his life, the death of his mother from ovarian cancer, the plan to bring troops home from Iraq, his dating of Michelle Robinson before they married, his views on parenting, and what music is on his iPod (rock, jazz, and classical). Banks not only asked Obama questions, she also played basketball with him and talked about how he keeps fit (treadmill and basketball). At one point, Banks asked Obama to look into a crystal ball and tell her what he saw in his future. His answer was, "The White House."[13]

Later, when Obama went on to win the Democratic nomination, Banks told an interviewer, "When Barack won the nomination, I just started bawling. I started calling all these people, and everybody was talking to me like I was crazy. They're like, 'Well, he hasn't won yet,' but I'm like, 'Yes, he has, because he's gotten this far.' I think he gives everybody so much hope."[14] Obama would go on to become the forty-fourth president of the United States after beating Republican nominee John McCain in the November 2008 election.

In January 2008, Banks had Democratic presidential candidate Hillary Clinton on her show. The two women talked about Bill Clinton's past affair with former White

Here, Banks sits down with Senator Barack Obama on her talk show during his run for the presidency in October 2007. Banks suggests he gives a crystal ball to his wife, Michelle, to celebrate their fifteenth wedding anniversary. When Banks asks what he sees in the crystal ball, Obama replies, "I see the White House right there."

House intern Monica Lewinsky, a topic Clinton has rarely spoken about in interviews. Clinton told Banks that during that entire time of the affair, she never doubted her faith or Bill's love for her. Later in the interview, Banks asked Clinton if she ever felt lonely. Clinton responded, "I don't feel lonely, but I do feel sometimes isolated. Because when you are in these positions that I have been in, it can be very isolating. It is one of the reasons I put on the dark glasses and the baseball cap and go out of the White House. President Harry Truman once said that the White House was like the crown jewel of the American penal system because you can feel confined."[15]

In February 2008, Republican presidential hopeful and former Arkansas governor Mike Huckabee appeared on the talk show. At the start of the interview, Banks brought up Huckabee's impressive weight loss (he had lost 110 pounds, or 50 kg). He discussed his former poor eating habits and lack of exercise and his new, healthy diet and running for exercise. Banks was complimentary of his success and sympathetic to the effort it took to get there.

After a commercial break, Banks turned the conversation to homosexuality. Banks is openly supportive of the gay and lesbian community. When interviewing Huckabee, she asked him specific questions to pinpoint his views on homosexuality. When Banks asked him if he believed that homosexuality is immoral, he replied, "I think that we were created to have relationships with people of the opposite gender. . . . I've had people who are gay that worked on my staff. It's not like I'm some homophobe. If you ask me, Is it the normal pathway? I don't think so. But, you know, I respect that people have different views about that."[16] When Banks asked him if he was comfortable with or opposed to changing the rules about marriage to include gay marriage, Huckabee responded, "Opposed."[17] Banks told Huckabee, "I'm asking you so many questions about this because I love the gays and the gays love me. And I know I cannot walk down the street here in New York City if I didn't press that issue and truly ask you that."[18]

At the end of the interview, Banks again lightened the mood by inviting Huckabee to play his electric bass guitar (he plays in a band called Capital Offense). To the delight of the audience, Huckabee taught Banks how to play a few notes; then he went on to play a bass solo. The Huckabee interview highlights Banks's ability to put her guests at ease even when she may not agree with their political beliefs or values.

Loving Your *Self*

Cycle 8 of *America's Next Top Model* began airing in February 2007. Natasha Galkina was the Cycle 8 runner-up, and Jaslene Gonzalez was the Cycle 8 winner. Gonzalez, from Chicago, Illinois, became the first woman of Puerto Rican decent to win the top spot. More than 6 million viewers tuned in to watch the Cycle 8 season finale—a record audience for *America's Next Top Model* and for CW.

The actual filming of Cycle 8 had begun at the end of 2006. Banks was on location in Sydney, Australia (also the contestants' international travel destination), in December 2006. During filming, paparazzi took photos of Banks on the beach wearing a one-piece swimsuit from unflattering angles that were published in tabloids and posted on the Web. Headlines (including "America's Next Top Waddle" and "Tyra Porkchop") spoke of Tyra being fat. Articles claimed she weighed 200 pounds (90.7 kg). (She in fact weighed 160 pounds, or 73 kg.)

REACTING TO THE PRESS

Banks told the *Guardian*, "If I was embarrassed or ashamed or had lower self-esteem, I would have hid. I would have just looked at those pictures and said, 'Oh my gosh, I want them to go away.'"[1] She then met with *People* magazine in January 2007 to talk about her weight gain that had been the talk of tabloids and Web site blogs for months. Although Banks was 30 pounds heavier than she had been two years earlier, she told *People* that she was happy with her figure and the way she looked. What she worried about was the not-so-subtle message the tabloids were sending to people larger than herself. If Banks was "fat," how were these people going to feel about their bodies? Banks felt the media—which blitzed young people with a barrage of magazine covers featuring rail-thin models—was once again sending the wrong kind of message.

Shortly after her interview with *People*, Banks dedicated an episode of her talk show to her weight gain. She came on the show wearing the one-piece swimsuit she had been photographed wearing in Australia. She struck poses on stage, giving the audience and the world full views of her body—from both flattering and unflattering angles.

She told the audience and viewers at home, "Luckily, I'm strong enough and I have a good enough support system. I love my Mama, and she has helped me to be a strong woman so I can overcome these kinds of attacks, but if I had a lower self-esteem, I would probably be starving myself right now. That's exactly what is happening to other women all over this country."[2] Later, holding back tears, Banks looked squarely into the camera and challenged "all of you that have something nasty to say about me . . . [about] women who've been picked on, women whose husbands put them down . . . or girls in school. I have one thing to say to you: Kiss my fat [expletive]!"[3] At the end of the show, Banks got emotional and began to cry. She told the *New York Times*, "I was very nervous—I had to do the first 15 minutes of the show in just my bathing suit, which was hard. And then I cried at the end. I was worried that the crying seemed weak, but the producers told me to leave it, that all women are vulnerable."[4]

The episode became an instant Internet hit on YouTube. People around the world began discussions about defining "fat" and "skinny." Two months after the "Kiss my fat [expletive]" episode ran in February, Banks launched a "So What" campaign to promote positive body images. She wanted to help women learn to love themselves for who they are—regardless of their weight. In one episode during the "So What" campaign, Banks and all the audiences members wore bright red T-shirts with their weight marked in stark white numerals across the fronts. Before a commercial break, Banks stood among the audience members and told them all to rip the numbers off the front of their shirts, saying "so what" to how much they weigh. Not long after Banks's "So What" campaign, Banks was listed as one of *People*'s "100 Most Beautiful People."

CONTINUED SUCCESS

The year 2007 marked the tenth anniversary of Tyra Banks's cover shot with *Sports Illustrated*. To celebrate Black History Month and her 10-year anniversary, Banks took part in a re-creation of the original cover shot. Banks intentionally tried on the same red and white polka dot bikini she had worn 10 years prior, knowing that because her body had changed in the past decade, she would need adjustments made to the suit. To the top portion of the bikini, stylists added some fabric on the sides. On the bottom portion, they let out the seams for a smooth fit.

In addition to the shoot with *Sports Illustrated*, Banks continued to appear occasionally on magazine covers. In August 2007, she appeared on the cover of *Ebony* magazine with Iman, Alek Wek, and Kimora Lee Simmons. In July 2008, Steven Meisel photographed Banks for an all-black issue of Italian *Vogue*. In September 2008, Alexi Lubomirski photographed Banks for the cover of *Harper's Bazaar*. On a spread inside, Lubomirski photographed Banks imperson-ating Michelle Obama. Also that month, Sebastian Faena photographed Banks alone and with Sessilee Lopez, an up-and-coming supermodel, for *V*.

AMERICA'S NEXT TOP MODEL: CYCLES 9 THROUGH 11

The fall season of Cycle 9 of *America's Next Top Model* brought several firsts. Banks, never having been a smoker, banned smoking among the contestants on the show. She also brought on environmentally friendly transportation for

IN HER OWN WORDS

Tyra Banks knows that every woman is beautiful in some way. She says:

> [E]very woman has to find something beautiful about her-self. Find one thing in the mirror you're proud of. At least one. Some women have problems finding just one. And sometimes we just get too caught up in comparing our-selves to other people.[5]

Tyra Banks at an NBA basketball game between the New York
Knicks and the New Jersey Nets at Madison Square Garden in
New York City, on April 16, 2007.

the contestants when they traveled to and from their photo shoots. Also for the first time, the cycle featured a contestant, Heather Kuzmich, who suffers from Asperger syndrome, a form of autism that affects verbal communication and social interactions. Kuzmich said of her experience on the show, "I thought I wouldn't be able to get along with any of the girls—I'd be too different—and since I've been here, I've learned so much. I learned to be more confident and I plan to not always be so self conscious. . . . I think the experience is much more than a prize."[6] The contestants traveled to China for their international destination. Although Kuzmich was a favorite, Chantal Jones was the Cycle 9 runner-up, and Saleisha Stowers was the Cycle 9 winner.

America's Next Top Model aired its tenth cycle in February 2008, which also included the show's one hundredth episode. The international destination for these 14 contestants was Italy—the same country used in Cycle 2. Also, longtime judge Twiggy did not appear in Cycle 10 because of scheduling conflicts. Czech supermodel Paulina Porizkova replaced Twiggy. Porizkova was well known in the fashion industry and had appeared on the cover of *Sports Illustrated*'s swimsuit issue in 1984 and again in 1985. She had also appeared on another popular reality television show, *Dancing with the Stars*, in 2007.

In this cycle, Anya Kop took runner-up, and Whitney Thompson took the win. In addition to a six-page spread in *Seventeen*, the management and representation by Elite Model Management, and the contract with Cover Girl, Thompson won a billboard in New York City's Times Square displaying her Cover Girl ad. Thompson became the first full-figured competitor to win *America's Next Top Model*. Thompson told an interviewer, "I've already heard online from boys and girls all over the world who are dealing with eating disorders. They're thanking me for standing up and saying, 'I am a plus-size model and I am beautiful.'"[7]

For Cycle 11 of *America's Next Top Model*, which started airing in September 2008, contestants traveled to the Netherlands for their international destination. Although Cycle 11 maintained 14 contestants, it was the first season in which a transgender contestant, Isis King, took part. King explains, "I was born physically male, but mentally [and] everything else I was born female. Some people might say that I'm transgender, some people might say transsexual. Personally, I prefer 'born in the wrong body.'"[8] Executive

REDEFINING "BEAUTIFUL"

For decades, magazines and advertisements have featured ultra-thin, fair-skinned models to sell products. These models become the stereotypical image of "beautiful," as the form and shape of their bodies are presented as what is "in" or "hot." In reality, most women are not model thin. Women come in all shapes and sizes. Tyra Banks calls the stereotype into question; she wants to redefine beautiful. When she casts contestants for *America's Next Top Model*, she is not looking for the "typical" high-fashion model. She wants women with depth, with character, with an inner beauty that shines through to the outside. She wants to see differences among the contestants—different skin colors, different personalities, and different body types and weights.

Tyra Banks is considered by most people to be beautiful. Some think she was more beautiful when she was younger and thinner. Others think she is as beautiful now, just changed. Banks talked to *Entertainment Tonight*'s Mark Steines about her body: "I like my body, but my body is the sum of parts. I'll be honest; I don't love my legs, and my calves are too small for producer Ken Mok told the *Associated Press*, "I think the one message we always try to get out there, that Tyra always expresses, is you want to widen the spectrum of what is considered beautiful."[9] King was eliminated in episode 5. In the final episode, Samantha Potter was named runner-up, and McKey Sullivan was named the winner.

As of 2009, *America's Next Top Model* was CW's highest-rated show. Not only is it is shown in 15 different countries, but MTV runs marathons of *America's Next Top*

me, and my thighs are kind of thick, and my ankles are really skinny, and, you know, I don't necessarily love my stomach—not as firm as it used to be—and I've got cellulite on my butt, and I've got what'd you call 'back-fat' when my bra's on."[10]

From her experience in the fashion and entertainment industry, Banks knows that how her body looks is going to directly affect her career. Yet she has managed to overcome that to some degree. She was about 20 pounds (9 kg) heavier than most models of her time, but she still managed to book jobs and sell products. She knows that the intensity of her eyes and the warmth of her smile are two of her most captivating features, and she worked hard to use those to her advantage.

Banks went on to tell Steines, "I look at [these aspects of my body] and I don't like it all the time, but I am fortunate enough to be from the fashion industry and know how to dress to hide those types of things. That's what I do on 'The Tyra Show' all the time, is tell women how to camouflage and hide things and accentuate the good."[11] Banks wants young women to start to see that *beautiful* is not synonymous with *perfect*.

Model. Despite the show's popularity and success, however, the fashion industry questions the validity of the concept of discovering America's next "top model": None of the winners from any cycle have made it big in modeling.

Banks is not bothered by the criticism. She knows she is selling a show, first and foremost. She told an interviewer, "Of course I know what a supermodel looks like, but I also know that a show filled with thirteen girls that have the right look and no personality is not going to be relatable or watched. I'm more interested in fighting for the racial mix of the cast."[12] There are few nonwhite high-profile models out there working, and Banks is trying to change that. Banks told the *New York Times*, "Dark-skinned black girls are usually not famous—if you think of black girls, it's light-skinned girls like me or Beyoncé or Halle Berry. When I'm casting a dark-skinned black girl on 'Top Model,' I'm sending a message to the little girl watching at home that she is beautiful."[13]

PERSONAL LIFE

Tyra Banks lives a relatively quiet life, despite her hectic work schedule. She has publicly announced that she does not drink alcohol and she does not use drugs. Although her work fulfills her, she does not feel the same way about her home life. With no husband, no children, and just a few

DID YOU KNOW?

Tyra Banks rarely wears just her own hair. She often wears wigs or weaves or adds extensions. She enjoys the freedom of being able to change her hair color, length, and style on a whim.

friends, she once told *Essence* magazine that she sometimes feels empty when she comes home from work. When asked what kind of man she is looking for, Banks opened up to *Ebony* magazine: "Someone who is very independent, a good provider so that he won't need any of my money, very loving, a giver, a supporter of me. Someone I can call in the middle of the night and cry, and he'll wake up and be there for me. He'll also open up and be vulnerable."[14]

Banks prefers to keep her private life private and does not talk to the media about her relationships. Over the years, she has dated on and off, but does not comment when reporters ask for details or try to make something more out of a friendship than it is. To one reporter, she explained, "I won't say if I'm single or dating or married or divorced. There's boundaries."[15] Still, Banks has had three longer relationships that she has not managed to keep from the media. The first was with director John Singleton. Then she later had another three-year relationship with basketball star Chris Webber, who then was playing for the Sacramento Kings. This relationship ended, however, in the early 2000s. More recently, Banks was dating Wall Street investment banker John Utendahl.

Regardless of whether Banks has a man in her life, she tries to keep a balance between work and recreation. If she did not, her work could easily consume her. Because Banks's work keeps her incredibly busy, and even though she so wholeheartedly throws herself into her various projects, Banks knows the importance of stepping back. She told an interviewer that "it is so important to take time for you[rself] and I don't think enough busy women do that. I go to the spa; I love reflexology. I love body scrubs and when they throw water on me like I'm a wild animal in the field. I don't work on the weekends; I go to the movies on the weekends."[16] In fact, Banks catches the release of nearly every American movie when it comes out. She also loves television and counts on her TiVo to catch all her favorite shows, including *Curb Your Enthusiasm*.

Perhaps surprising to some, given her high-fashion background, Banks is not interested in designer clothes and does not enjoy putting an outfit together. Her stylist comes to her apartment and creates several outfits for her to choose among. On television, she frequently wears low-cut dresses, but at the office she mostly wears jeans and T-shirts or blouses. She generally wears clothes on her shows and at the office that are within her audience's budgets. In fact, after the taping of every episode of *The Tyra Banks Show*, the show's Web site posts a photograph of Banks and lists purchasing information on everything she was wearing.

Banks is a warm, outgoing person who values her small, tight circle of good friends. She stays close with her family and leans on them for support, friendship, and advice. When she is working, Banks stays focused and dedicated. She plays two distinctly different roles—the stern and judgmental yet caring and understanding host of *America's Next Top Model*, and the playful girl-next-door host of *The Tyra Banks Show*. When working at her production company and on the sets of projects that she produces, Banks stays organized and efficient. When she is at home or with friends, Banks can finally relax and be whatever fits her mood at the time. She told one reporter, "Some days I want to be serious. Some days, I want to act the fool and have a great time."[17]

THE MOVE TO NEW YORK

At the end of 2007, Banks moved *The Tyra Banks Show* from Los Angeles to New York. Banks said of the move, "I'm thrilled to be moving to New York. . . . Moving the talk show to New York provides a great opportunity to meet all kinds of people and keep sharing the message of

Banks enjoys a laugh with her mother at her mother's home on December 29, 1993. The strong support she received from her mother has helped her throughout her career.

empowerment with everyone everywhere. The excitement of New York City will translate to the show each and every day as we continue to face compelling issues . . . head on."[18] Banks still operates Bankable Productions at its home on the Warner Brothers lot back in California, but she opened Bankable Enterprises in New York City. As she explained to an interviewer, "[Bankable Enterprises] is more corporate, dealing with things that are not television or film-based."[19] She told the *New York Times*, "I prefer the pace and excitement of New York to Los Angeles. I feel so alive in New York—the city seems to fuel my brain."[20]

Banks takes pride in her many creative projects and likes to stay involved in most areas of her business enterprises. She told an interviewer from *Pink*, "In the past it was about being the talent and waiting for the phone to ring. Now I'm the creator and the producer. I make things happen."[21] Banks, however, gives careful consideration to the substance and merit of each project and does not take on new ventures simply to try something out. She told *Pink*, "One thing that's important to me is not doing something just to make money. We'll be doing things we stand by, things we create."[22]

As a producer, Banks continues to impress and surprise. The president of CBS, Leslie Moonves, told an interviewer, "I have to admit, I didn't really expect [Banks] to have this kind of drive or creative ability. But I realized what a great producer she was when my daughter, who was then in college and is my best focus group, told me that *Top Model* was her favorite show. I underestimated Tyra. I think we all did."[23]

Opening
New Doors

People in the entertainment industry no longer underestimate Tyra Banks and what she can do. The *Hollywood Reporter* listed Tyra Banks as No. 36 in a list of "The Power 100 Women in Entertainment." Banks has proven to be a force and shows no signs of slowing down. She regularly appears on talk shows to promote her own shows or films or discuss her philanthropic work with TZone or a particular charity event. Banks has appeared on *The Daily Show with Jon Stewart*, *Live with Regis and Kelly*, *The Early Show*, *The Tonight Show with Jay Leno*, *The Ellen DeGeneres Show*, *Larry King Live*, *Late Night with Conan O'Brien*, *The View*, *Today*, and *Entertainment Tonight*.

A MOGUL IN THE MAKING

In April 2008, the five hundredth episode of *The Tyra Banks Show* aired. This meant a lot to Banks, as many people had warned her when she started the show that it would likely get canceled. Few daytime talk shows last more than one season. *The Tyra Banks Show* had lasted three and was still going strong. Banks, once again, had proved skeptics wrong.

For the milestone show, Banks took her audience and television viewers on a trip down memory lane. She showed clips from her first three seasons, including some of her favorite moments. She also brought back some past guests whose lives had changed as a result of being on her show. Then Banks played a segment taped on the streets of New York City. In it, Banks spoke with *American Idol* winner Clay Aiken, who was in New York for his starring role in the Broadway musical *Spamalot*. A lucky Aiken fan had the opportunity to meet Aiken in person. Aiken also gave each studio audience member tickets to *Spamalot*.

Later in the show, in front of a New York City subway station in Union Square, Banks co-hosted a segment with *America's Next Top Model* winners Jaslene Gonzalez (from Cycle 8) and Saleisha Stowers (from Cycle 9) and recent contestant Claire Unabia (from Cycle 10). The guests were all wearing T-shirts that said "Top Citizen." Banks and the "Top Citizens" gave makeover tips to 10 girls who had been previously selected from a nearby McDonald's. Conducting the interviews on the street with the volunteers from McDonald's (similar to the work Banks had done on Oprah Winfrey's program), Banks used her flamboyant, girlfriend-style of interview to set the tone for the segment—relaxed, playful, and fun.

Banks also took her "Top Citizens" on a walk to meet with New York City mayor Michael Bloomberg. Together, Banks, Bloomberg, Gonzalez, Stowers, and Unabia planted a tree (which Banks named "Model Oak"). The planting was part of Bloomberg's campaign to plant one million trees across the city. After the ceremonial planting, Bloomberg declared April 18, 2008, to be "The Tyra Banks Show Day." In Bloomberg's proclamation, he stated, "Tyra's style, generosity, and ferocity truly represent the very best our great city has to offer. On behalf of all New Yorkers, here's hoping that her 'Made in New York' show will continue creating episodes 'all new from the 212' (and 718, 646, 917, and 347) for many years to come."[1]

RECOGNITION FOR A JOB WELL DONE

The Tyra Banks Show has steadily increased its number of viewers each year. At the start of 2008, it was reaching 6 million national viewers weekly. Telepictures president McLoughlin told an interviewer, "[Banks] has an Everywoman feeling to her and relates to people—she's surprising that way. You don't expect a supermodel to be someone you can feel a connection to. It turns out she has this authentic quality."[2]

Banks's authentic quality brings people together. She reaches all age groups and all races. CBS's Leslie Moonves told the *New York Times* that "the television audience in general is becoming increasingly colorblind, and younger viewers are particularly colorblind. It's similar to the pattern we're seeing with voters and Barack Obama—he and Tyra have a similar appeal to the youth audience."[3]

On June 20, 2008, Banks attended the Thirty-fifth Annual Daytime Emmy Awards, held at the Kodak Theatre in Los Angeles, California. *The Tyra Banks Show* had been nominated, along with *Dr. Phil* and *A Place of Our Own*, for Outstanding Informative Talk Show. Banks came to the awards show wearing a beige, made-to-order dress designed by Georges Chakra. Banks's mother was at the ceremony, too.

Banks accepts the award for outstanding informative talk show for *The Tyra Banks Show* at the Daytime Emmy Awards in Los Angeles, California, on June 20, 2008.

After Banks was named the winner of the Emmy, she told the crowd, "I want to thank Oprah Winfrey for her inspiration. She is the queen and will always be the queen." She also thanked her mother, who was crying with happiness in the audience, and her show's entire crew.

RECENT PROJECTS

Banks continues to lead a busy life. Her vice president of Bankable Enterprises, Bradford Sisk, told an interviewer, "[Banks] looks at 24 hours differently than most people. Tyra doesn't sit still for a minute. Her brain is always going. If she's not focusing on one project, she's thinking up the next one."[4] Banks is ambitious, creative, and willing to work. She is constantly thinking of new ideas to develop into a television show or some other project.

To help her keep track of the details of these projects, Banks used a BlackBerry device. When she started feeling hand cramps from using it too often, however, she went back to notebooks (similar to the ones she used when starting out in Paris). Now she keeps a notebook with her at all times to jot down notes to various people. She told an interviewer, "Everybody on my team has a tab. There's a 'Top Model' tab, talk-show tabs, different assistants have tabs, a Bankable tab. I write things down in the middle of the night, and when I see the person, I turn to their tab and I read to them."[5]

Banks created a new reality television show, *Stylista*, in which 11 contestants compete for a one-year paid editorial position as an assistant to Anne Slowey, the fashion news director of *Elle* magazine. In addition, the winner receives a year's clothing allowance from H&M (a Swedish clothing company) and a one-year lease on a New York apartment. The prizes total a value of $100,000. The show premiered in September 2008 immediately following *America's Next Top Model* on CW. Banks herself does not appear on the show; she is an executive producer of *Stylista* through Bankable Productions. Warner Horizon Television also produces the show.

On the show, Slowey comes across as a tough, hard-to-get-along-with boss, but Slowey's reputation in the industry is the opposite. The *New York Times* noted: "Ms. Slowey ought to receive a reality-TV acting Emmy for playing a much more intimidating version of herself."[6] And yet it is, in part, Slowey's demanding personality that makes the show interesting. "Part of the appeal of a show like 'Stylista' is that it resurrects a long-vanished way of office life, one filled with rules and regulations, distinct hierarchies and dress codes and nothing as fuzzy as flex time. As Ms. Slowey succinctly explains to the contestants at the outset: 'To be in my world you either get it or you don't.'"[7]

Slowey works with *Elle*'s creative director, Joe Zee, to decide which contestant gets "fired" each week. The 11 contestants were Arnaldo, Ashlie, Cologne, Danielle, Devin, DyShaun, Jason, Johanna, Kate, Megan, and William. When it was down to the remaining three contestants (DyShaun, Johanna, and Megan), their final challenge was an interview with the editor in chief of *Elle* magazine, Robbie Myers. Following the interview, Megan was immediately eliminated.

DyShuan and Johanna were then instructed to style a celebrity and direct her in a photo shoot for the cover of *Elle*. Previously eliminated Ashlie, Danielle, Kate, and Megan returned to assist DyShaun or Johanna with this final project. Twenty-eight-year-old Johanna, with her impeccable attention to detail, ultimately won the editorial position at *Elle*.

Banks then executive-produced another project, *The Clique*, with Warner Premiere. *The Clique* is a film based on a series of best-selling books by Lisi Harrison about preteen girls surviving the difficulties of an all-girls private middle school. Having been both the "mean girl" and the "picked-on girl" herself in middle school, Banks understood the inner workings of cliques. She told *Entertainment Tonight*, "I identify with 'The Clique' personally, because I've been on both sides. I've been the queen bee . . . and I've been the

Contestants try to impress *Elle*'s fashion-news director Anne Slowey on *Stylista*, a reality show produced by Tyra Banks's production company.

girl that wants to be in it so badly, but is just so awkward [and] never will be."[8]

Liz Tigelaar wrote the screen adaptation, and Michael Lembeck directed *The Clique*. Ellen Marlow (playing Claire Lyons), Elizabeth McLaughlin (playing Massie Block), Samantha Boscarino (playing Alicia Rivers), Sophia Anna Everhard (playing Dylan Maril), and Bridgit Mendler (playing Kristen Gregory) star in the movie. This project did not appear in theaters; it was sold only as a DVD. Banks appreciated the mix of fun and seriousness the movie delivered. She told an interviewer, "The one thing I love about 'The Clique' is there's beautiful sugar and fashion and fun, but there's a message underneath it."[9] In November 2008, Banks brought the cast of *The Clique* on her talk show to promote the movie.

In addition to these projects, Banks was working on a reality television project called *True Beauty*. This time Banks would executive produce the show alongside former model and current actor/writer/producer Ashton Kutcher. *True Beauty* premiered in prime time on ABC in January 2009. Similar to *America's Next Top Model*, contestants live together in an apartment, take part in challenges, and then meet in a judging room—for this show, called the "Hall of Beauty." In the Hall of Beauty, one contestant is eliminated.

Contestants were playing for a cash prize of $100,000 and a spot in *People* magazine's "100 Most Beautiful People" issue. The judges for the show were former model Cheryl Tiegs and fashion celebrity stylist Nolé Marin, who was also a judge from *America's Next Top Model* Cycles 3 and 4. Actress Vanessa Minnillo, the winner of the Miss Teen USA pageant in 1998, hosted the show. The contestants were

❦ DID YOU KNOW?

Lifestyle entrepreneur Martha Stewart, with her worldwide name recognition, is one of Tyra Banks's heroes. Banks hopes that similarly to Stewart's fame, simply the name "Tyra Banks" will bring Banks's personality and style to mind. She wants people to think of Tyra Banks as tough, beautiful, empathetic, and empowering.

Ashley Michaelson, Billy Jeffrey, Chelsea Bush, CJ Miller, Hadiyyah-lah Sa'id, Joel Rush, Julia Anderson, Laura Leigh, Monique Santiago, and Ray Seitz.

In a twist quite unlike *America's Next Top Model*, however, these contestants believed they were competing in a competition based on their outer beauty alone. In fact, the judges were scoring their inner beauty as well as their outer beauty. Tiegs explained, "We have 54 cameras set up, we have a spy room so that we can see how they interact with the other contestants and how they act in the little tests that we put forth every week. . . . There were people who cared for the environment and some didn't. Some gave to charity, some didn't. So we were able to see all that, to see what kind of person they really were or are."[10] In addition to photo shoots, the tests the contestants faced each week challenged character traits, including honesty, generosity, teamwork, and modesty.

During the episode that generosity was tested, the contestants were first divided into three teams. Each team received $100 to purchase three complete outfits. Later, in the hidden-camera challenge, a woman at a charity collection table asked for donations to help her charity. The contestants who donated part of the money they had received "passed" the test; those who did not donate (Bush, Michaelson, Santiago, and Seitz), "failed."

In the final episode, the three remaining contestants (Anderson, Jeffrey, and Rush) took part in a photo shoot wearing only a towel. After that challenge, back at the apartment, a clue written in a note directed them to the spy room. Anderson, Jeffrey, and Rush were told the truth behind the competition and shown clips from the season at their lowest inner-beauty moments. Later, at the Hall of Beauty, Tiegs, Marin, and Minnillo discussed each contestant's strengths and weaknesses of both their inner and outer beauty. They revealed that Jeffrey was the second runner-up. Rush was the runner-up, and Anderson took the title "True Beauty."

MOVIE PROJECTS

Banks worked on a couple of films in 2008 and 2009. She had a cameo appearance in the comedy movie *Tropic Thunder*, which was released in August 2008. The film, starring Ben Stiller, Jack Black, and Robert Downey Jr., pokes fun at Hollywood and films about the Vietnam War. Ben Stiller both wrote (along with Justin Theroux and Etan Cohen) and directed the movie. *Rolling Stone* called *Tropic Thunder* "killer smart, lacing combustible action with explosive gags."[11] Banks brought Stiller and Black on her show for an interview to promote the film the month it hit theaters.

In April 2009, *Hannah Montana: The Movie* appeared in theaters. The Disney movie, directed by Peter Chelsom, starred Miley Cyrus. Banks had a small role in the film. She flew to Tennessee to shoot her scene. Here, at the CoolSprings Galleria Mall, Banks, playing herself, fights with Cyrus's character, Hannah Montana, over shoes in a department store. Although Banks's demanding schedule with her television shows does not allow her much time for filmmaking, her cameo appearances in movies, however, work well given her time constraints and her desire to be a part of the movie industry.

What's Next for Tyra Banks?

As a model and actress, Tyra Banks has graced runways, magazine covers, advertisements, television, and film. With her highly rated television programs—reality show *America's Next Top Model* and talk show *The Tyra Banks Show*—Banks is easily recognizable around the world. Banks, however, is not merely prominent in front of the camera. She has a savvy business sense, a down-to-earth personality, a strong work ethic, and a desire to help young women discover their own inner beauty and strengths.

As we have seen, Banks was not always successful. She was not always pretty. Tall and skinny as a preteen girl, she felt awkward and out of place. In high school, she grew into her tall frame and her beauty became apparent. Still, modeling agencies repeatedly turned her away. Banks could

Banks behind the camera during a photo shoot on *America's Next Top Model*. Pictured behind her is Jay Manuel.

not book a job. Banks evolved, however, from withdrawn and unsure to bold and confident. Once primarily known for her modeling, Tyra Banks is now known worldwide as being much more than a pretty face—she is a competent and determined businesswoman who is making a dramatic impact on the entertainment industry.

In 2008, Tyra Banks earned an estimated $23 million from her television shows. Her net worth is estimated to be about $75 million. Banks told *Entertainment Weekly*, "Oprah Winfrey is a mogul. Martha Stewart is a mogul. I'm probably a mogul in the making. I'm almost there."[1] Peter Roth, the president of Warner Brothers television, noted, "Very few people have the vision, the passion, and the ambition that [Tyra Banks] does. In a marketplace this cluttered, anytime you have a presold brand or persona, it gives you a leg up. And she is a presold commodity."[2]

Banks clearly has a mission: "I'm passionate about inspiring people to fulfill their own dreams and fantasies through entertainment that is engaging, uplifting, and of course, fun! This is *my* dream realized."[3] Through her work with her TZone Foundation and her television programs, Banks has inspired countless young girls to take responsibility for and control of their lives.

Tyra Banks does not expect to remain in front of the camera forever. As she told the *New York Times*, "It won't always be my face. I know that nothing lives forever, and I'm prepared for that. But there's no end to producing. I'll still be at the helm."[4] She has set herself up to do just that. Banks relishes expanding her businesses and hopes to explore merchandising, real estate development, and perhaps a Tyra Banks magazine. Banks's all-consuming drive and energy will undoubtedly help her to achieve these goals. Banks admitted to one interviewer, "I once had an ex-boyfriend tell me that I was 'so independent' . . . like it was the deepest insult. . . . I'm just an overachiever. I don't take vacations. My work ethic is a little obsessive."[5] Yet it is because of this obsessive work ethic that Tyra Banks thrives.

CHRONOLOGY

1973   Tyra Lynne Banks is born on December 4 in Inglewood, California.

1990   Banks signs with Elite Model Management.

1991   Banks graduates from Immaculate Heart High School; she is discovered by a modeling scout and offered the opportunity to model in Paris.

1991–1993   Banks models haute couture in Europe.

1992   Banks establishes the Tyra Banks Scholarship at Immaculate Heart High School.

1993   Banks begins her commercial modeling career; she appears in a recurring role on *The Fresh Prince of Bel-Air*.

1994   Banks named as one of the "50 Most Beautiful People in the World."

1995   Banks signs a five-year contract with Cover Girl; she appears in her film debut, *Higher Learning*.

1996   Banks becomes the first African American to appear (with Valeria Mazza) on the cover of a *Sports Illustrated* swimsuit issue; she is named as one of the "50 Most Beautiful People in the World."

1997   Banks becomes the first African American to appear solo on the cover of a *Sports Illustrated* swimsuit issue; she receives the Michael Award for Supermodel of the Year.

1998	Banks authors the book *Tyra's Beauty Inside & Out*, and becomes a Victoria's Secret Angel.
1999–2001	Banks works as an apprentice youth correspondent on Oprah Winfrey's talk show.
1999	Banks organizes a camp for girls called TZone; she creates her own production company called Tygirl Incorporated. (She later changes the name to Ty Ty Baby.)
2000	*Sports Illustrated* names Tyra Banks Woman of the Year.
2002	Banks develops the idea for *America's Next Top Model*.
2003	Banks changes the name of Ty Ty Baby Productions to Bankable Productions.
2005	Banks turns TZone into a public charity called the Tyra Banks TZone Foundation; she retires from modeling and launches *The Tyra Banks Show*. Banks walks her last Victoria's Secret Fashion Show.
2008	Banks wins the Daytime Emmy for Outstanding Informative Talk Show at the Thirty-fifth Annual Daytime Emmy Awards; she produces *Stylista* and *The Clique*.
2009	Banks produces *True Beauty* with Ashton Kutcher.

NOTES

CHAPTER 1: GOODBYE TO RUNWAY

1. Hirschberg, Lynn, "Banksable," *New York Times*, June 1, 2008.

CHAPTER 2: SOUTHERN CALIFORNIA GIRL

1. Hirschberg, Lynn, "Banksable," *New York Times*, June 1, 2008.
2. "An Empire Behind the Scenes: Tyra Banks, Talk-show Host and Producer, on Her Life in Front of and Behind the Camera," *Newsweek*, October 13, 2008.
3. Ferguson, Euan, "The Supermodel Turned Spokeswoman," *Guardian*, April 15, 2007.
4. Ibid.
5. Hirschberg, "Banksable."
6. "An Empire Behind the Scenes."
7. Hirschberg, "Banksable."
8. "The Shotcaller: John Casablancas." *Complex Magazine*. http://www.complex.com/CELEBRITIES/shotcaller/John-Casablancas.

CHAPTER 3: HIGH FASHION IN EUROPE

1. Hirschberg, Lynn, "Banksable," *New York Times*, June 1, 2008.
2. Ferguson, Euan, "The Supermodel Turned Spokeswoman," *Guardian*, April 15, 2007.
3. "Tyra Banks." *People*. http://www.people.com/people/tyra_banks.
4. "An Empire Behind the Scenes: Tyra Banks, Talk-show Host and Producer, on Her Life in Front of and Behind the Camera," *Newsweek*, October 13, 2008.
5. Hirschberg, "Banksable."
6. Ibid.

7. Ibid.
8. Walden, Celia. "Patrick Demarchelier: 'I Don't Like Exhibitionist Women. . .'" *Telegraph*, September 1, 2008. http://www.telegraph.co.uk/fashion/3365143/Patrick-Demarchelier-I-dont-like-exhibitionist-women....html.
9. Adato, Allison, "Tyra Talks," *People* 67, no. 5 (February 5, 2007).
10. Ferguson, "The Supermodel Turned Spokeswoman."
11. Hirschberg, "Banksable."

CHAPTER 4: BREAKING NEW GROUND IN COMMERCIAL MODELING

1. Fernandez, Maria Elena, "Banking on 'Phase Two,'" *Los Angeles Times*, November 8, 2005.
2. Gregory, Deborah, *Essence*, February 1995, p. 60.
3. "The Shotcaller: John Casablancas." *Complex Magazine*. http://www.complex.com/CELEBRITIES/shotcaller/John-Casablancas.
4. Gates, Anita, "Film Reviews: Love Stinks," *New York Times*, September 10, 1999.
5. Moore, Claudia. "Review of *Tyra's Beauty Inside and Out*." *School Library Journal*. http://www.amazon.com/Tyras-Beauty-Inside-Tyra-Banks/dp/0060952105/ref=sr_1_1?ie=UTF8&s=books&qid=1238076100&sr=1-1.
6. King, Jennifer Carolyn. "Angelic 2005 Victoria's Secret Fashion Show: Getting 'in the Spirit.'" Rugged Elegance Web site, December 7, 2005. http://www.ruggedelegantliving.com/a/003850.html.
7. Watson, Margeaux, "Tyra on Top: She's Regal, Real, and Telling All—or Most of It, Anyway," *Suede*, April 2005.

8. Hirschberg, Lynn, "Banksable," *New York Times*, June 1, 2008.

9. Ferguson, Euan, "The Supermodel Turned Spokes-woman," *Guardian*, April 15, 2007.

10. "An Empire Behind the Scenes: Tyra Banks, Talk-show Host and Producer, on Her Life in Front of and Behind the Camera," *Newsweek*, October 13, 2008.

CHAPTER 5: *AMERICA'S NEXT TOP MODEL* IS BORN

1. Norment, Lynn, "Tyra Banks: On Top of the World—African American Fashion Model," *Ebony*, May 1997.

2. Williams, Paige, "Banking on Banks," *Pink*, January/February 2008.

3. "Supermodel Tyra Banks, Host and Producer of 'America's Next Top Model' and New Syndicated Talk Show, 'The Tyra Banks Show,'" *Jet*, December 26, 2005.

4. Ebert, Roger. "Love & Basketball." *Chicago Sun-Times*, April 21, 2000. http://rogerebert.suntimes.com/apps/pbcs.dll/article?AID=/20000421/REVIEWS/4210304/1023.

5. Crust, Kevin, "Quick, Somebody, Turn the Light Out," *Los Angeles Times*, July 15, 2002.

6. "Tyra Banks: Tyra Tears Up as She Remembers 9/11." Contactmusic.com, December 9, 2006. http://www.contactmusic.com/news.nsf/article/tyra%20tears%20up%20as%20she%20remembers%20911_1007951.

7. Hirschberg, Lynn, "Banksable," *New York Times*, June 1, 2008.

8. Blakeley, Kiri, "Tyra Banks On It," *Celebrity 100*, July 3, 2006.

9. Ibid.

10. Watson, Margeaux, "Tyra on Top: She's Regal, Real, and Telling All—or Most of It, Anyway," *Suede*, April 2005.

11. Fernandez, Maria Elena, "Banking on 'Phase Two.'" *Los Angeles Times*, November 8, 2005.

12. Christian, Margena A., "Tyra Banks: Creator of TV's 'America's Next Top Model' Tells Why Singing Is Her Next Move," *Jet*, March 1, 2004.

13. Ibid.

14. Williams, "Banking on Banks."

15. Blakeley, "Tyra Banks On It."

16. Watson, "Tyra on Top."

17. Tuccillo, Andrea. "Eva Pigford." TheCinemaSource. com. http://www.thecinemasource.com/celebrity/ interviews/Eva-Pigford-Model-Behavior-interview-348-0.html.

18. Watson, "Tyra on Top."

19. Fernandez, "Banking on 'Phase Two.'"

CHAPTER 6: *THE TYRA BANKS SHOW*

1. The Tyra Banks TZone Foundation, "TZone Story." http://tzonefoundation.org/tzone-story/.

2. The Tyra Banks TZone Foundation, "TZone Updates." http://tzonefoundation.org/tzone-updates/.

3. The Tyra Banks TZone Foundation, "TZone Story."

4. Hirschberg, Lynn, "Banksable," *New York Times*, June 1, 2008.

5. Ferguson, Euan, "The Supermodel Turned Spokeswoman." *Guardian*, April 15, 2007.

6. Hirschberg, "Banksable."

7. Ibid.

8.   Ibid.

9.   "Supermodel Tyra Banks, Host and Producer of 'America's Next Top Model' and New Syndicated Talk Show, 'The Tyra Banks Show,'" *Jet*, December 26, 2005.

10. Blasberg, Derek. "I Called Her Mahogany." *V* magazine. http://www.vmagazine.com/article.php?n=11319.

11. Gay and Lesbian Alliance Against Defamation news release. "GLAAD Announces Nominees, Special Honorees for 20th Annual GLAAD Media Awards presented by IBM." http://www.glaad.org/media/release_detail.php?id=4936.

12. Hirschberg, "Banksable."

13. Ibid.

14. Brown, Laura. "American Dream: From the Runway to the Oval Office, Everything Is Possible for Tyra Banks." *Harper's Bazaar*, September 2008. http://www.harpersbazaar.com/magazine/cover/tyra-banks-interview-0908.

15. Frederick, Don, and Andrew Malcolm. "Hillary Clinton Feels the White House Is Like a Prison." *Los Angeles Times*, January 20, 2008. http://www.latimes.com/news/nationworld/nation/la-na-ticket20jan20,1,5613382.story?track=rss.

16. "The Tyra Banks Show" with Mike Huckabee, February 29, 2008.

17. Ibid.

18. Ibid.

CHAPTER 7: LOVING YOUR *SELF*

1.   Ferguson, Euan, "The Supermodel Turned Spokeswoman," *Guardian*, April 15, 2007.

2. "Tyra Banks Stands Up to Critics of Her Weight." *People*, February 1, 2007. http://www.people.com/people/article/0,,20010424,00.html.

3. Brown, Laura. "American Dream: From the Runway to the Oval Office, Everything Is Possible for Tyra Banks." *Harper's Bazaar*, September 2008. http://www.harpersbazaar.com/magazine/cover/tyra-banks-interview-0908.

4. Hirschberg, Lynn, "Banksable," *New York Times*, June 1, 2008.

5. Ferguson, "The Supermodel Turned Spokeswoman."

6. Rocchio, Christopher. "Heather Kuzmich the Ninth Girl Cut from 'America's Next Top Model 9'" Reality TV World, November 29, 2007. http://www.realitytvworld.com/news/heather-kuzmich-ninth-girl-cut-from-america-next-top-model-9-6184.php.

7. "Whitney Thompson Named *America's Next Top Model*." US Magazine, May 15, 2008. http://www.usmagazine.com/Whitney-Thompson-Named-Americas-Next-Top-Model.

8. "Transgender 'America's Next Top Model' Contestant Speaks, Works It." *New York*, August 14, 2008. http://nymag.com/daily/fashion/2008/08/video_transgender_americas_nex.html.

9. Bland, Bridget. "Transgender on TV: Laverne Cox & Isis King Brings On New Reality." BlackVoices.com, October 2, 2008. http://entwire.blackvoices.com/2008/10/02/transgender-on-tv-laverne-cox-and-isis-king-brings-on-new-reality/.

10. "Tyra Banks on Body Image." ET Online. http://www.etonline.com/news/2007/10/55309/.

11. Ibid.

12. Hirschberg, "Banksable."

13. Ibid.
14. Collier, Aldore, "The Joys & Perils of Being a Top Model," *Ebony*, May 2004.
15. Keveney, Bill, "Tyra Fans Might Do a Double-take on TV," *USA Today*, October 2005.
16. Blasberg, Derek. "I Called Her Mahogany." *V* magazine. http://www.vmagazine.com/article.php?n=11319.
17. Keveney, "Tyra Fans Might Do a Double-take on TV."
18. Finn, Natalie. "Tyra Takes New York." E Online, June 6, 2007. http://www.eonline.com/uberblog/b55333_Tyra_Takes_New_York.html.
19. Blasberg, "I Called Her Mahogany."
20. Hirschberg, "Banksable."
21. Williams, Paige, "Banking on Banks," *Pink*, January/February 2008.
22. Ibid.
23. Hirschberg, "Banksable."

CHAPTER 8: OPENING NEW DOORS

1. The Tyra Banks Show. "Celebrate 'The Tyra Banks Show' Day." April 29, 2008. http://telepicturesblog.warnerbros.com/tyrashow/2008/04/celebrate_the_tyra_banks_show.php.
2. Williams, Paige, "Banking on Banks," *Pink*, January/February 2008.
3. Hirschberg, Lynn, "Banksable," *New York Times*, June 1, 2008.
4. Ibid.
5. Ibid.
6. Bellafante, Ginia, "It's a Fashionista War: Wear Armor," *New York Times*, October 21, 2008.
7. Ibid.

8. "On 'The Clique' Set with Tyra Banks." ET On-line, February 29, 2008. http://www.etonline.com/news/2008/02/59136/.

9. Ibid.

10. "Exclusive Interview: Cheryl Tiegs Has True Beauty." My Take on TV, January 5, 2009. http://mytakeontv.wordpress.com/2009/01/05/cheryl-tiegs/.

11. Travers, Peter. "Tropic Thunder." *Rolling Stone*, August 21, 2008. http://www.rollingstone.com/reviews/movie/18270126/review/22187117/tropic_thunder.

CHAPTER 9: WHAT'S NEXT FOR TYRA BANKS?

1. Stack, Tim. "Tyra Banks: America's Next Top Mo-gul." *Entertainment Weekly*. http://www.ew.com/ew/article/0,,20178169,00.html.

2. Ibid.

3. Tyra Banks bio. http://tyrashow.warnerbros.com/showinfo/bio.php.

4. Hirschberg, Lynn, "Banksable." *New York Times*, June 1, 2008.

5. Watson, Margeaux, "Tyra on Top: She's Regal, Real, and Telling All—or Most of It, Anyway," *Suede*, April 2005.

BIBLIOGRAPHY

Adato, Allison. "Tyra Talks." *People*, 67, no. 5 (February 5, 2007).

Banks, Tyra. "An Empire Behind the Scenes: Tyra Banks, Talk-show Host and Producer, on Her Life in Front of and Behind the Camera." *Newsweek*, October 13, 2008.

Bellafante, Ginia. "It's a Fashionista War: Wear Armor." *New York Times*, October 21, 2008.

Blakeley, Kiri. "Tyra Banks On It." *Celebrity 100*, July 3, 2006.

Bland, Bridget. "Transgender on TV: Laverne Cox & Isis King Brings On New Reality." BlackVoices.com, October 2, 2008. Available online at http://entwire. blackvoices.com/2008/10/02/transgender-on-tv-laverne-cox-and-isis-king-brings-on-new-reality/.

Blasberg, Derek. "I Called Her Mahogany." *V* magazine. Available online at http://www.vmagazine.com/article. php?n=11319.

Brown, Laura. "American Dream: From the Runway to the Oval Office, Everything Is Possible for Tyra Banks." *Harper's Bazaar*, September 2008. Available online at http://www.harpersbazaar.com/magazine/cover/tyra-banks-interview-0908.

Christian, Margena A. "Tyra Banks: Creator of TV's 'America's Next Top Model' Tells Why Singing Is Her Next Move." *Jet*, March 1, 2004.

Collier, Aldore. "The Joys & Perils of Being a Top Model." *Ebony*, May 2004.

Crust, Kevin. "Quick, Somebody, Turn the Light Out." *Los Angeles Times*, July 15, 2002.

Ebert, Roger. "Love & Basketball." *Chicago Sun-Times*, April 21, 2000. Available online at http://rogerebert.

suntimes.com/apps/pbcs.dll/article?AID=/20000421/
REVIEWS/4210304/1023.

"Exclusive Interview: Cheryl Tiegs Has True Beauty." My
Take on TV, January 5, 2009. Available online at http://
mytakeontv.wordpress.com/2009/01/05/cheryl-tiegs/.

Ferguson, Euan. "The Supermodel Turned
Spokeswoman." *Guardian*, April 15, 2007.

Fernandez, Maria Elena. "Banking on 'Phase Two.'" *Los
Angeles Times*, November 8, 2005.

Gates, Anita. "Film Reviews: Love Stinks." *New York
Times*, September 10, 1999.

Gregory, Deborah. *Essence*, February 1995.

Hirschberg, Lynn. "Banksable." *New York Times*, June 1,
2008.

Keveney, Bill. "Tyra Fans Might Do a Double-take on
TV." *USA Today*, October 2005.

Klum, Heidi. "Tyra Banks," *Time*, April 30, 2006.

Martin, Denise. "'Top Model' Duo Gets a 'Fabulous'
Spinoff." *Los Angeles Times*, November 19, 2008.

Norment, Lynn. "Tyra Banks: On Top of the World—
African American Fashion Model." *Ebony*, May 1997.

Ogunnaike, Lola. "My, What Pretty Claws." *New York
Times*, September 26, 2004.

"Supermodel Tyra Banks, Host and Producer of 'America's
Next Top Model' and New Syndicated Talk Show, 'The
Tyra Banks Show.'" *Jet*, December 26, 2005.

"The Shotcaller: John Casablancas." *Complex Magazine*.
Available online at http://www.complex.com/
CELEBRITIES/shotcaller/John-Casablancas.

"Transgender 'America's Next Top Model' Contestant Speaks, Works It." *New York Magazine*, August 14, 2008. Available online at http://nymag.com/daily/fashion/2008/08/video_transgender_americas_nex.html.

"Tyra Banks." *New York Magazine*. Available online at http://nymag.com/fashion/models/tbanks/tyrabanks/.

Tyra Banks bio. Available online at http://tyrashow.warnerbros.com/showinfo/bio.php.

"Tyra Banks: Tyra Tears Up as She Remembers 9/11." Contactmusic.com, December 9, 2006. Available online at http://www.contactmusic.com/news.nsf/article/tyra%20tears%20up%20as%20she%20remembers%20911_1007951.

The Tyra Banks TZone Foundation, "TZone Story." Available online at http://tzonefoundation.org/tzone-story/.

Watson, Margeaux. "Tyra on Top: She's Regal, Real, and Telling All—or Most of It, Anyway." *Suede*, April 2005.

Williams, Paige. "Banking on Banks. *Pink*, January/February 2008.

FURTHER RESOURCES

BOOKS

Hill, Anne E. *Tyra Banks: From Supermodel to Role Model*. Minneapolis: Lerner Publications Company, 2009.

Mitchell, Susan K. *Tyra Banks*. Pleasantville, N.Y.: Gareth Stevens Publishers, 2008.

Schweitzer, Karen. *Tyra Banks*. Philadelphia: Mason Crest Publishers, 2009.

WEB SITES

America's Next Top Model Web Site
http://www.cwtv.com/shows/americas-next-top-model

Official Tyra Banks Web Site
http://www.tyrabanks.com

The Tyra Banks Show Web Site
http://tyrashow.warnerbros.com

TZone Foundation
http://www.tzonefoundation.org

INDEX

ABOUT THE AUTHOR

ANNE M. TODD has a bachelor of arts degree in English and American Indian studies from the University of Minnesota. She has written more than 20 nonfiction children's books, including biographies on American Indians, political leaders, and entertainers. Todd is also the author of the following Chelsea House books: *Roger Maris*, for the BASEBALL SUPERSTARS series; *Mohandas Gandhi*, for the SPIRITUAL LEADERS AND THINKERS series; *Chris Rock* and *Jamie Foxx* for the BLACK AMERICANS OF ACHIEVEMENT, LEGACY EDITION series; *Vera Wang*, for the ASIAN AMERICANS OF ACHIEVEMENT series; and *Susan B. Anthony* and *Venus and Serena Williams* for the WOMEN OF ACHIEVEMENT series. Todd lives in Prior Lake, Minnesota, with her husband, Sean, and three sons, Spencer, William, and Henry.

PICTURE CREDITS

Page

10: Stephen Chernin/ AP Images
20: Studio Fernanda Calfat/ Getty Images Entertainment/Getty Images
26: Evan Agostini/Getty Images Entertainment/ Getty Images
28: Alan Levenson/Time Life Pictures/Getty Images
38: Christophe Ena/ AP Images
41: Ron Galella/ WireImage/ Getty Images
49: Mark J. Terrill/AP Images

52: Lester Cohen/ WireImage/Getty Images
67: CBS Photo Archive/ Getty Images
74: Warner Bros, Jason Kempin/AP Images
80: Seth Wenig/AP Images
87: Alan Levenson/Time & Life Pictures/Getty Images
92: Matt Sayles/AP Images
95: The CW/Photofest
100: ALISON LESSMAN/ THE CW/Landov